George Ja
HOLYOAKE'S JOURNEY of 1842

George Jacob HOLYOAKE'S JOURNEY of 1842

from
Birmingham to Bristol
and back again,
and those he met along his way

Catherine Howe

HISTORY INTO PRINT

First published by
History into Print, 56 Alcester Road,
Studley, Warwickshire B80 7LG in 2012
www.history-into-print.com

ISBN: 978-1-85858-340-2

A Cataloguing in Publication Record
for this title is available from the British Library.

Typeset in Galliard
Printed in Great Britain by
Berforts Group Limited.

Introduction

Instant fascination was my response when I first came upon George Jacob Holyoake's story while studying with the Open University in the 1990s. I started to read all I could find about him and, as I took down notes, it soon became necessary to start a narrative, and once the narrative was begun the notion of his walk from Birmingham to Bristol took over as a perfect way in which to bring together the events leading up to his trial and imprisonment in 1842.

During Holyoake's lifetime the British state and the Church of England together held a strangle-hold on the physical and moral lives of industrial workers. The Corn Laws made bread too expensive for working families to buy and they, having no vote, were powerless to vote these measures away. Many became Chartists or Socialists. Because of the effects of industrialization, independent artisans found themselves no longer independent but instead the blood and sinew, the living 'hands' of their masters' manufactories. Men and women, even teenage boys and girls, were transported to penal colonies for years for stealing the means to live, and too often the Justice of the Peace was a Church of England minister. Prevailing political and economic philosophies did not allow for woolly social policies. Workers became statistics, and the established church provided no challenge to this notion.

My aim in writing this short book has been to explore those people and events which influenced George Jacob Holyoake's journey to the point of his trial and imprisonment at Gloucester, and to put his experience as much as possible within the context of the world about him. It was a world in which a great and controversial Church of England bishop could say of England that religion "is the sole foundation on which the Government stands. The whole frame of society rests upon religion". For all his life, George Jacob Holyoake was one who tirelessly tested this belief.

Malvern
January 2012

God is our guide! No swords we draw,
We kindle not war's battle fires;
By reason, union, justice, law,
We claim the birth-right of our sires:
We raise the watch-word liberty;
We will, we will, we will be free!

George Loveless -
Methodist preacher and Tolpuddle Martyr

1

In a hall on Rockingham Street, Sheffield, on a Sunday evening in January, 1842, George Jacob Holyoake stood before a group of working men and women who had gathered there to hear him speak. He was twenty-four years old. In the crowd might have been a police officer or two, for this was a gathering of socially suspect characters. The young Holyoake was to speak in his capacity as a social missionary, posted to Sheffield by an organisation known as the Universal Community Society of Rational Religionists which paid him a small salary for spreading socialist propaganda amongst the working classes and for instructing them in mathematics, geology and philosophy. He did other teaching to supplement his income. The Universal Community Society of Rational Religionists was not a religious organisation, it was a social reform movement which had a network of offices extending throughout the country and had been founded by Robert Owen, a man with a reputation for utopian ideas. Owen was also an inspiration to many working men and women who saw hope for themselves in his social schemes and who gave their time and energies to the Owenite cause. George Jacob Holyoake was one of these.

Holyoake was a native of Birmingham and it was there, two years before the scene at Sheffield, that he had met and befriended a young Londoner, Charles Southwell, who had also been drawn by the appeal of Owen's organisation to become one of its social missionaries. Charles Southwell was now in prison having been arrested at Bristol some weeks earlier for publishing anti-religious papers, an event which had left the young Holyoake thunderstruck. Now, as his friend faced his first of twelve months inside Bristol gaol, Holyoake stood before the Sheffield assembly and, with some courage as the crowd, he knew, might well contain local authority informers, said to his listeners:

> I may be told that christianity [*sic*] repudiates persecution which is a violation of its principles, but after the exceptions for 1800 years have

> formed the rule, I beg leave to doubt it. Christianity repudiate persecutions foresooth! Where are the christian men who will raise their voices against it – where are the pulpits from which it will be denounced?... I was born pious, and nursed in orthodoxy, and have been, till within a very short period of this, a believer in the humanising tendency of Christianity: but the persecution of my friend... has been within these few weeks, the cradle of my doubts and the grave of my religion. My cherished confidence is gone, and my FAITH IS NO MORE. [1]

It was faith in church creed and the power of prayer that was 'no more'. Southwell's arrest had irrevocably turned Holyoake against orthodox church authority. This falling away from religion had not come suddenly to Holyoake but from the accumulated effects of events spanning most of his twenty-four years. He was a rational young man and his natural inclination to reason was quite ready to take the place of his religious belief: 'As revelation means something superadded to reason, we cannot be said to possess it, for reason has to determine what is, and what is not revelation, and therefore is superior to it', he wrote at the time.[2] Holyoake was soon to make a journey which would change his life in ways beyond his choosing and which would mark a point of significant change in British history.

* * * * *

George Jacob Holyoake was born on the thirteenth of April, 1817, within sight of the spire of Birmingham's St. Martin's Church, within the very streets of the industrial revolution, 'born with steel and books in my head' he said.[3] He was the second child, first son of George and Catherine Holyoake. His birth coincided with a time when two men, one by 1842 already a significant influence on Holyoake and the other soon to be, were enthusiastically inviting the disapproval of polite society upon themselves. The first of these, Robert Owen, horrified his friends as completely as he delighted his enemies when, in the August of 1817 at the London Tavern on Bishopsgate, he spoke publicly against all religions, a gross error he called them, which was a reckless thing to do in those days when the church exercised great social power. The other, Richard Carlile, was busy selling copies of the radical pamphlet the *Black Dwarf*, published by Jonathan Wooler, and was working towards the first of many prison terms he would serve for similar acts. Times were hard, social discontent and radicalism so vigorous in the year of Holyoake's birth that a Tory government lead by the Earl of Liverpool suspended the Act of Habeas Corpus. This had prompted the otherwise irrepressibly bold William Cobbett, considered by a number of establishment figures to be a highly pernicious influence on society, to flee the country in March, with his two young sons, for America. Samuel Romilly described the parliament of the day as being 'regardless of the liberties and rights of the people, and of the principles of general justice'.[4] Holyoake never was to forget that he had been born 'when social and political ideas were in the air', and derived much satisfaction from the fact. [5]

As a child and youth, Holyoake gave himself over whole-heartedly to work, study and self-improvement. The religious element in his upbringing came from his mother, Catherine, and her father Richard Groves. The little boy might often be seen escorting his grandfather through the leafy environs of St Martin's churchyard in Birmingham as he discharged his duties as beadle, which, to the child's mind, mainly consisted of checking the condition of the graves and grounds thereabout. His mother, on the other hand, would take him each Sunday to a dissenters' chapel. Her choice for many years was John Angell James' Congregational Church at Carrs Lane. As a young boy, the wonders of religion captured Holyoake's imagination, the local baker looked a lot like God he thought and, more profoundly, impressions of the modesty and charm of his grandfather at prayer stayed with him for life. He was to grow away from such things but throughout his long life it was morality and ethics which absorbed his energies.

Some reckoned this moral sense to be generated by an impassive rigidity in his make-up, especially in his later years.[6] His memoirs show how ruled he was by an overwhelming impulse to right all he considered as wrongs, a trait which did not always work in his favour, and this tendency was often brought to bear on slights to himself, of which there were a number. He dreaded being misjudged or thought egotistical, and in an attempt to avoid this he tended towards pedantry and a controlled manner. The pleasure he later would find in the company of prominent men and women is regarded, by some, as evidence of a disappointing weakness in his character, but pretended nonchalance was not one of his failings. Few would deny his fair-mindedness.

By the time of his speech at Sheffield, George Jacob Holyoake was a married man, the father of two infant daughters, and he was ambitious to change the world. He nonetheless resigned his position as social missionary in the spring of 1842 and returned to his family in Birmingham, probably just in time for his twenty-fifth birthday. By mid-May he was ready to visit Charles Southwell, now entering into his fifth month of imprisonment at Bristol. Holyoake set out, on foot, from his Birmingham home on Sunday morning, the 22nd of May, with a walk of ninety miles ahead of him. In his pockets were some lecture notes, may be a book or two, some bread. He would eat when food came his way. 1842 was a year of exceptionally good weather, and the bright morning would have lifted his spirits as he went along the road. The streets of Birmingham extended only as far as Edgbaston Park to the south-west and he would soon leave these behind as he headed into open countryside. His way along the Bristol Road took him past the garden his grandfather had once cultivated and where the old man and he, years ago, had spent quiet and peaceful hours together. It was a place which, when he was a child, had seemed to him a 'paradise of fruit, and flowers, and vegetables'.

His final destination was the less bucolic Cumberland Road gaol at Bristol where Charles Southwell was serving his sentence for blasphemy. Having six months earlier written an article full of vitriol on the Old Testament, Southwell had been arrested and imprisoned. Holyoake and a like-minded sympathiser, Maltus Ryall who lived in London, were among the very few who had supported Southwell during his trial. The two had exchanged letters on the subject, the most recent from Ryall containing the offer of work in London if Holyoake would come there.

This was an undreamed of opportunity for the young man but he had kept to his Bristol plan, probably in loyalty to Southwell and because he was engaged to give a lecture, part-way through his journey, at Cheltenham, on the principles of 'Socialism'.

Southwell, during his earlier days in London, had achieved the distinction of debating with one of Holyoake's heroes, Richard Carlile. Holyoake, on the other hand, had never seen London let alone met Carlile so when he and Charles Southwell first met at Birmingham in 1840 Southwell must have held no small degree of fascination for the younger man. They were very different from one another. It was a friendship of attracted opposites. Holyoake was temperamentally steadier and better mannered than his friend. For one thing, he respected his opponent's point of view in debate, Southwell was for a combative style which would carry his point. And where the cautious Holyoake might rebel, soon recklessly enough, in the cause of Truth and Free-thought, Southwell was a rebel by principle, he was not a diffuser of conflict and seemed always to end up bloodied.

In 1841 Charles Southwell produced a paper called *The Oracle of Reason* the purpose of which was to advocate atheism 'as freely as ever Christianity was dealt to the people'. Privately, Southwell doubted that 'such a paper will be permitted by the authorities of this country'.[7] The offending article penned by Southwell and which appeared in the fourth number of *The Oracle*, led to his arrest. 'The Bible', he wrote, is a 'revoltingly odious Jew production' which:

> has been for ages the idol of all sorts of blockheads, the glory of knaves, and the disgust of wise men. It is a history of lust, sodomies, wholesale slaughtering, and horrible depravity; that the vilest part of all other histories, collected into one monstrous book, could scarcely parallel! Priests tell us that this concentration of abominations was written by a God; all the world believe priests, or they would rather have thought it the outpourings of some devil! [8]

This issue of *The Oracle of Reason* also carried an article on the Theory of Regular Gradation, an early evolutionary theory, and a passage on Symbol Worship. It was a nicely printed paper, each issue generally carrying two well executed engravings. Southwell's piece is not to be read as an anti-Semitic diatribe, although suspicion of British Jews was endemic in these days. It offended because it attacked the English churches and their dependence on a literal reading of the Bible. For his efforts he was taken from his bed in the middle of a November night by the Bristol authorities and, bail refused him, was kept to a cell in solitary confinement for seventeen days.

Holyoake never subscribed to his friend Southwell's sensationalist style of journalism but he did not hesitate to ally himself with the principle of this author's bellicose piece and, in Southwell's absence, agreed to step in as editor of *The Oracle*. Richard Carlile, irresistibly drawn to the activity, now wrote to him from London, asking, 'What is all this splutter and clatter about god?':

> You, Southwell, and others, are now where I once was, resting upon the mere flippant vulgarising of what you and the world consent to call atheistic Infidelity, regulating your amount of wisdom by a critical contrast with other people's folly. Nothing that you say leads to any settlement of the dispute between you and them. [9]

It was not, however, the influence of Southwell's views or tactics so much as the events surrounding his arrest and imprisonment that turned Holyoake into an anti-religionist. His fury at the treatment handed out to his friend by the magistrates at Bristol did not subside over weeks. Before Southwell could be brought to trial, a friend of the persecuting body, one John Brindley, 'anticipating', Holyoake fumed, 'the malignant joy of his friends', led the way by addressing letters to Southwell's judge, 'prejudging his case, claiming his condemnation, proposing his punishment and feasting with demonic avidity, most truly christian [*sic*], on his prospective suffering'. [10]

This is how things stood with Holyoake in the weeks before he set out to walk to Bristol. His religious faith, already tested through experience of life on the streets of industrial Birmingham, had given way to deistic rationality. Southwell's trials at the hands of churchmen finally unravelled his belief in Christianity as a model of human behaviour. By the time of his journey to Bristol no sympathy remained in him for the system, or 'The Thing', as William Cobbett called it.

There was tremendous risk to him in publicly supporting Charles Southwell for the young Holyoake was not protected by any social standing. His father worked at the great Eagle Foundry on Broad Street, Birmingham, and although the son liked to dwell upon an independent, artisan inheritance, the family now worked for a master by the skill of its hands. George Holyoake, the father, was a whitesmith, and, in the words of his son, a 'comely' man, not given to much self-expression and who had a natural dignity. Before he turned to Socialism, Holyoake had worked for thirteen years by his father's side and had had ample opportunity to observe how 'when summoned by his employers he always walked up without uncovering his head, as was usual with others. His not doing so seemed natural to him. It was not disrespect', Holyoake wrote, 'it was self-respect'.[11] His father's natural dignity, not derived from religious feeling, would go deep with the boy and influence his thoughts and manner for the future. His father's way was not to mention religion, he seems never to have spoken for or against it, so it is surprising how willingly Holyoake was to fall in with a noisy firebrand like Southwell.

He was walking, not riding, to Bristol, because he had no money. Now that the position he had held at Sheffield was ended, he could barely manage to support himself, his wife and two infant daughters. And so he paced out along the dirt road on that May morning, a young, slim and dark haired figure, with no greater prospect than to see his friend Southwell kept in a prison cell for speaking against a religious institution which, he had come to think, deserved every condemnation it received. Considering the distance Holyoake was prepared to walk, anyone would think him a robust, hearty sort of young man. In fact, he had been a sickly child, always aware of friendly doubts about his ability to survive this world for long. Now, at the age of twenty-five, he was not unattractive to look at. He wore a full, dark moustache and had a well-shaped nose and forehead. His voice, though, was a disappointment, both to himself and to others, for it was high pitched, shrill and feeble some said, and a drawback to a man ambitious to spread social propaganda.

A phrenological assessment had been made of Holyoake's head four years earlier when he assisted George Combe, a man famed for his work in the field of phrenology which was a popular and, then, respected science claiming to enabled the practitioner to tell the character of an individual by feeling the contours of the subject's head. Combe had come to Birmingham in the May of 1838, to give two weeks of lectures and demonstrations on the subject. This episode in Holyoake's youth produced an event which would bring out a peculiar trait in him, pertinent to the story ahead, and which was directed at Combe himself. Holyoake so hated to be misunderstood or thought ill of that throughout his life he was driven to repair the slightest harm done to his reputation. To be thought badly of by anyone would spur him on to energetic acts of self-vindication, sometimes years after the event. Even, sometimes, when it was entirely unnecessary. What happened was this.

It was back in 1838 that the twenty-one year old Holyoake, already teaching mathematics at the Birmingham Mechanics' Institution, was introduced to George Combe by the Institution's senior tutor, William Hawkes Smith. George Combe was known to Holyoake as the author of *The Constitution of Man*, a book on practical ethics which had fascinated the younger man. Hawkes Smith's idea, having already been put to and rejected by Holyoake's friend Frederick Hollick on pecuniary grounds, was that he might assist Combe in the fourteen lectures he had prepared to give at the Birmingham's Philosophic Institution. The famous man and twenty-one year old met one evening in late May. As Holyoake relates:

'Mr. Hawkes Smith introduced me to Mr Combe, saying friendly words as to what he believed to be my intelligence and fitness; whereupon I said, "These kindly assurances are not necessary in Mr Combe's case, as he, by a more certain process, can judge himself of my suitability"'. At this he bared his head so that Combe might pass his hand over it. A smiling Combe declared that Holyoake 'would suit him well'. Payment was not mentioned.

As it turned out, the assistant's duties took up some four hours each night as well as a course of morning manipulations. Combe's gesture of gratitude to the willing Holyoake at the end of the lectures comprised 'an old bust, by De Ville, with the nose broken off, which would not go into his box', but which Holyoake valued as coming from him, 'more than any other bust with the nose on, and that would go into a box'.[12] Like others of a similar temperament, his enthusiasm for the moment and the man was greater than for his pocket, but this trait was not shared by most of his young friends at the Mechanics' Institution, who later asked what Combe had given him for his services. Holyoake had expected nothing and had received nothing. When William Hawkes Smith heard of this, he wrote to Combe on Holyoake's behalf. Combe replied that his young assistant 'had no claim upon him' and had assisted during the lectures not entirely to his satisfaction.

It might have been happier had the matter been left there, but Holyoake, his honour now slighted, was persuaded to write a further letter to George Combe, by this time departed for America, with assurances that he had never asked for payment but that friends thought he had the right. This letter was to be carried to Mr Combe in Boston by a well-wisher and put into his hands there. Holyoake never received a reply to his second letter and so carried its copy about with him, ready to deliver it personally to Mr Combe should an opportunity ever arise. He carried it for eight years before he was able to relieve himself of it at an event in Glasgow. 'I think your conscientiousness will induce you to correct what you have… asserted' he writes to Combe, '…Hoping you will take an early opportunity of correcting *at least the remarks* you have applied to me'.[13]

At Glasgow, Combe assured Holyoake that 'nothing remained in his recollection the least injurious' to the young man's reputation.[14] This appeased Holyoake and brought to an end an episode which reveals his great need to seek vindication when embarrassed. It was a trait which would rule him for life.

2

Holyoake's plan was to make his journey to Bristol in three stages. He would stop off at Worcester for a night, maybe two, before going on to Cheltenham where, on the evening of May 24th, he was engaged to give a lecture at the Mechanics' Institution on "Home Colonization as a Means of Superseding Poor-Laws and Emigration". This communitarian philosophy was the ground rock of the Rational Religionist Society's doctrines, a philosophy expounded by Robert Owen who, since publicly declaring his own anti-religious sentiments in the year of Holyoake's birth, had lived a life of varying successes. After Cheltenham, Holyoake planned to walk on to Bristol to see Southwell.

The walk from Birmingham to Worcester is some twenty-five miles. Once past the Bristol Road gardens and over the Griffin Brook, he would be into Worcestershire and faced with an ascent of the Lickey Hills. The Lickeys, rich with quartz, rise up from the plateau on which Birmingham stands then fall some nine hundred feet, southerly, towards Bromsgrove and the wide Severn plain. On these open heights where linnets flew, the temperature can be three or four degrees colder than on the fertile lands below. Westward from these summits the Waseley meadows fall, the Clent Hills rise, onwards to Stourbridge.

The countryside was already cut through with railways, Liverpool to Manchester, Manchester to Birmingham, Birmingham to London and Gloucester. Nine years earlier a prototype steam carriage, with some thirty passengers, had caused a sensation by journeying from Birmingham to Coventry at a steady speed of eight miles an hour, failing in its return journey up the Lickey incline. Holyoake records in his Log Book that he had gone with his father to witness this miracle. Coventry lies a few miles off to the south-east from the Clents, and there, on this first morning of Holyoake's journey, an embryonic George Eliot, Marion Evans, was preparing to walk to church with her father. For Miss Evans this was no small matter for she had refused to attend church service since Christmas. Her winter of 1842, as with Holyoake, had been spent anguishing over her religious beliefs. In February she had written to her father, saying that although she admired the Hebrew Bible and:

> ... much of what I believe to have been the moral teaching of Jesus himself, I consider the system of doctrines built upon the facts of his life... to be most dishonourable to God and most pernicious in its influence on individual and social happiness. [1]

Which was a much politer way of saying very much what Charles Southwell had said in *The Oracle of Reason.* Marion Evans was a friend of George Combe. His phrenological assessment of her was that she had a very large brain and that her temper was nervous lymphatic. He also observed that she was rather tall, delicate in health, and 'showed great analytic power and an instinctive soundness of judgment'.[2] In May 1842 Holyoake was ignorant of her existence and she of his. Had they known each other then, there would have existed between them some sympathy. They were destined to be acquainted and later in life Holyoake delighted in recalling how, when he was editor of the *Leader* and she editor of *The Westminster Review*, (both presses were near neighbours on Fleet Street), she would fondly call him "the Providence of the Office".

Once off the Lickey Hills and heading towards Bromsgrove, Holyoake would have the exquisitely pleasurable sight of freshly leafed hedgerows which, according to an earlier observer:

> ... are well stored with elm timber, the largest, finest, and, I believe, best in the Kingdom, growing lengthy, fine, and large, and being generally sound and hearty, free from shakes and flaws... the county is interspersed, in various parts, with coppices of oak of different degrees of growth. [3]

The roads bounded by these hedgerows were made up of soil and the cuttings of vegetation roughly covered with assorted stones and gravel. In his ears would be the sound of his own boots stepping out, also the noise of any nearby human industry carrying well on the early morning air, and that of birds. In the pause between the sound of other road traffic, all else would be quite quiet.

The grass lands and meadows into which Holyoake was descending from the Lickeys were considerable:

> The Vale of Severn contains, very probably, ten thousand acres of a deep rich soil, in some places as level as can be conceived... Upon the land great

> numbers of sheep and cattle are fatted. The county is intersected in all directions with smaller rivers, brooks, and rivulets; whose margins consist of good meadow and pasture... The soil originally, from the rich upland, has a fertility, and gives the grass a staple, which affords a nutriment to cattle, superior to what is given by the same herbage in poorer countries. [4]

The principal pasture herbage of the Vale of Severn and Avon numbered 'ray-grass; white clover, trailing trefoil, barley-grass; timothy-grass; crested dog's tail; sedge-grasses; vernal grass, meadow fox-tail; flote grass; tall fescue; creeping bent grass; marsh fox-tail; meadow soft grass; brome grass; meadow burnet; meadow-vetchling; bird's-foot trefoil; creeping crow-foot; orchard-grass; quake grass, besides some other coarser grasses, neutral plants, meadow flowers, and weeds'.

Multitudes of hedge sparrows, or shufflewings as some called them, flitted in and out of every hedgerow, and as Holyoake made his way down from the heights towards Bromsgrove, around about him would dart bull-finches filching the early germs of garden gooseberries, cherries and green gage plums.

Years before, John Angell James, Birmingham preacher and Holyoake's erstwhile religious mentor, had taken this road with his wife on the day of their wedding. A great storm had broken over the newly-weds' heads and their postilion had taken shelter under a tree. James recalled how:

> Aware of our danger in such a situation, I ordered him to proceed, but as the storm increased he again took shelter under another tree, and, upon being remonstrated with, he declared that the hail was so heavy, that neither he nor the horses could stand under it... It was an awful moment; the thunder was rolling, the lightning flashing, and the hail, notwithstanding the protection of the tree, fell so heavy that it seemed as if the roof of the chaise would be beaten in. [5]

As a boy Holyoake would be taken by his mother, Catherine, to John Angell James's Congregational Chapel at Carrs Lane to hear that preacher address his flock from the high pulpit there. Carrs Lane Chapel had been rebuilt in 1819 and was now a large brick building with a 'lofty and imposing cemented front in the pseudo Grecian style within which were placed the entrances' and although this design was considered by some to be inappropriate to a place of worship for dissenters, it was held in great affection by its incumbent.[6] The new building could accommodate more than two thousand worshippers. John Angell James attracted

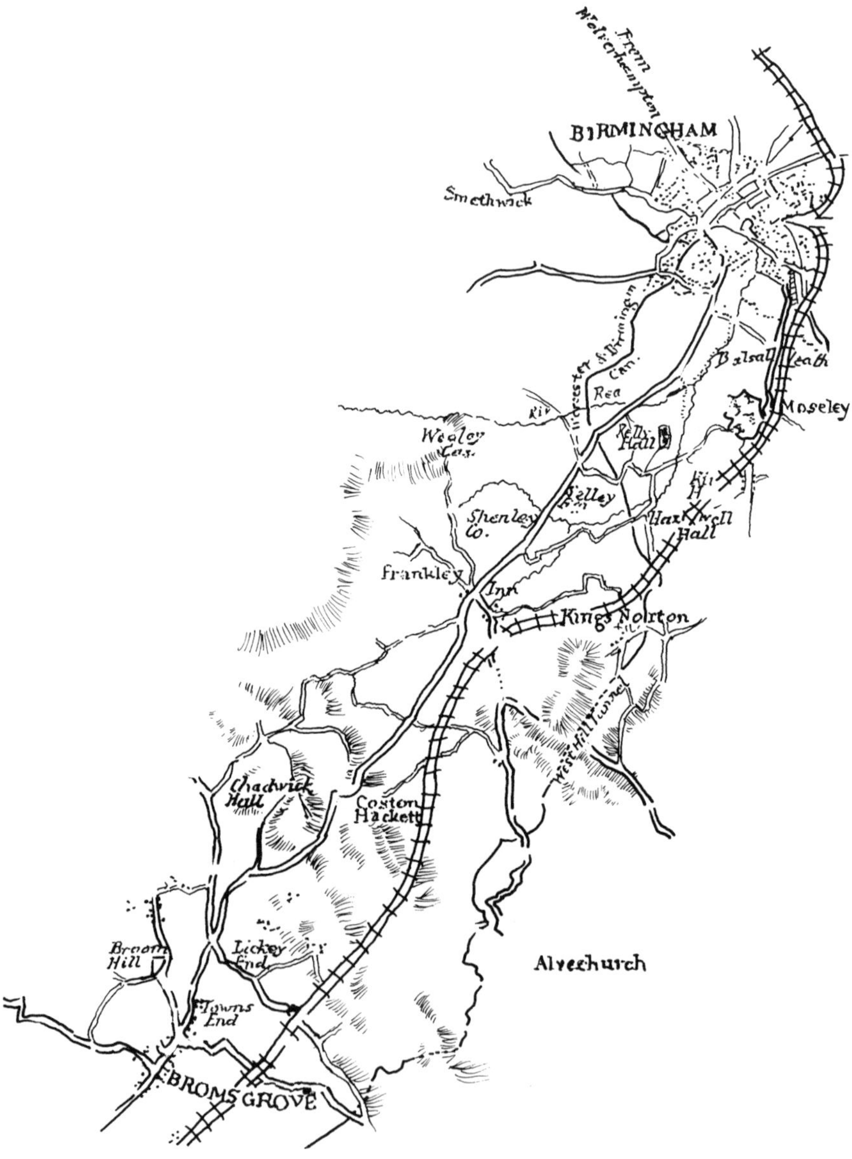
From Wolverhampton
BIRMINGHAM
Smethwick
Worcester & Birmingham Can.
Balsall Heath
Rea
Riv
Moseley
Weoley Cas.
Shenley Co.
Frankley
Inn
Kings Norton
Hazlewell Hall
West Hill Tunnel
Chadwick Hall
Coston Hackett
Broom Hill
Lickey End
Towns End
Alvechurch
BROMSGROVE

large congregations each Sunday for his voice was much admired. His successor to the Carrs Lane Ministry says of it that 'for sweetness, richness, and pathos' it was rarely equalled, 'never surpassed, and which even then was as absolutely under his control as in his later years'.[7] He was a master of 'the grand pulpit manner', and 'the simplicity and pathos of his prayers' would 'magnetize his hearers'.[8]

"It is not enough to know your *actual sins*" James would tell his congregation, which included Catherine Holyoake and her son George, "you must also clearly understand your *original sin and inherent depravity of heart*",[9] and, delivered in repetitive prose favoured by evangelical preachers of all ages: "What turned Adam and Eve out of paradise? Sin. What destroyed God's own city, and scattered his chosen people as vagrants over the face of the earth? Sin. What brought disease, accidents, toil, care, war, pestilence, and famine into the world? Sin."[10]

John Angell James was an enthusiastic man who, aware of his own shortcomings, had learned some discretion in later years. Like Holyoake, he had first come to his religion through his mother who was inclined to pray loudly. Mrs. James was a woman of 'sweet, peaceable, and gentle disposition', her son recalled:

> a general favourite, and deservedly so, but not possessed of an enlarged mind. She was a woman of sincere piety, without much theoretical knowledge. Her heart was beyond her head, as is the case, I believe, with many of God's children. She was a woman of prayer, and so fervent in her private devotions, that she could be heard far beyond the precincts of her closet.[11]

Born in Blandford Forum in 1785, the young John Angell James was a trouble to his pious mother and fit for nothing but fighting according to contemporaries. His education was a desultory affair, and he was sent, when thirteen years old, to serve as apprentice to a linen-draper in Poole where he was encouraged in religious feeling by the example of a fellow apprentice who would kneel to pray each evening at his bedside in spite of ridicule from his peers. James saw the moral courage in this act; he was inspired, enquired further and fell under the influence of a Calvinist. His religious mentor was a local cobbler who lived in a room 'not more than eight or ten feet square', in Fish Street. It was here that James developed his abiding interest in things ecclesiastical although he as yet 'had very crude notions of justification and other great doctrines of the New Testament', and he was still novice enough to be tempted by the pleasures of the temporal world.

> I was betrayed by curiosity into… inconsistency, and that was to go and see a mimic play, got up by a few young men of the town. While in the room, my conscience so severely reproved me, that its accusations were like scorpion stings. I was situated under a large beam, and I trembled through my whole frame lest it should fall and crush me to death: as soon as I could, I left the place and jumped for joy when I found myself safe on the outside of the house. I mention these things to prove that there may be a work of grace going on in the soul when some appearances in young converts would lead us to suspect the reality of the change.[12]

His was a religion of feeling as much as of the intellect and, like his mother, allowed his feelings 'so far to get the upper hand of my judgement as to pray so loud, that though I was in the attic I was heard in the lower parts of the house'. He was inclined to weep under the influence of a good sermon delivered by a mellifluous voice, and was to remain a spiritual enthusiast. At that point in religious life when Holyoake was to pause and turn away, James' pace and appetite increased. He embarked upon a ministerial education with the Gosport Congregationalists where he saw a danger in supplanting the natural feelings with learning. Personal piety 'without great care', he later wrote, 'is flattened, and learning is sometimes gained at the expense of godliness'.

> I remember that when I entered the college the class were in the middle of the system of divinity, and the first lectures I had to copy, to read upon, and to study, were on "The Freedom of the Will"; and one of the first books I had to read was Jonathan Edwards' celebrated treatise on this profound question. […] To a youth just leaving the counter, with no previous habits of study, who had gone through no process of mental training, such a volume should prove a most vexatious and discouraging commencement: it was indeed a *pons asinorum* to my untutored brain, which, to tell the truth, I did not, and could not pass over, so I tumbled over the side of the bridge into the water, and, narrowly escaping drowning, scrambled up the bank and got into the road again, with the rest of the train, a little further on. [13]

Some twelve years before Holyoake's birth James, already in his twentieth year, arrived for the first time at Birmingham. He was youthfully insensible to the purpose of his visit which was to test his suitability as a minister for Carrs Lane

Chapel. He met the rigours of his candidature with enviable nervelessness: 'I was going to preach', he says, 'and that was all'. At that time Carrs Lane Chapel was shared by the Congregationalists with the Baptists. James, 'self-possessed to an unusual degree for so young a man', was not put out by this first experience of preaching, and acquitted himself well during the few sermons he gave over the following weeks. So it was not long before, with a squeeze of the hand, and a screwed up mouth, his host smilingly asked him to take up the post of minister, which he did in 1805.

His first years in Birmingham turned out to be surprisingly difficult. The nervelessness with which he had confronted his trial period did not last, and James suffered a physical collapse in the year of Holyoake's birth, an event which he suspected was caused by anxiety. He writes of that year of 1817:

> it pleased God to visit me with a most alarming bodily illness, in the form of a low fever, which deprived me of the use of my limbs for a considerable time, and left me so enfeebled that I was nine months out of my pulpit. [...] I was always of a nervous temperament. It has through life been the besetting fault of my constitution. I have ever been prone to look on the dark side of events, and to prognosticate by my fears, rather than my hopes. [14]

So as James lay ill in his bed, Catherine Holyoake lay, some streets away, giving birth in hers, to the child in whom the Calvinist-inspired James would instil the tenets of evangelical Christianity as experienced in the early nineteenth century.

There were seats available at Carrs Lane Chapel for three hundred Sunday School scholars of which George Jacob Holyoake was one. He says he learned nothing during the five years he attended there, between the ages of ten and fifteen. All knowledge that did not derive from Christian piety was assiduously avoided. Any criticism of the Bible was kept from young ears. James advised the parents of his Sunday School children to keep the poetry of Scott, Southey, Wordsworth, Coleridge and Tennyson well away from their offspring. Of Byron he is reported to have said, 'he wrote as with the pen of an archangel, dipped in the lava which issues from the bottomless pit'. [15]

John Angell James was the true offspring of eighteenth century evangelical revivalism which lived by the atonement, justification by faith, the infallibility of the Bible, and Hell for those who did not believe. This is what the children of Carrs Lane Sunday School learned. Holyoake said he learned nothing there but that was after the event. At the time he soaked up his lessons for he was an earnest and eager boy and a good subject for religious conversion. He half believed John Angell James had wings tucked under his coat.

He and his fellow pupils probably sang a hymn popular at the time which went:

> There is a dreadful hell,
> And everlasting pains,
> Where sinners must with devils dwell,
> In darkness, fire and chains. [16]

Children were to believe this and Holyoake did, for a while. But as he grew he read, and once he reached the wider and sunnier shores of the Mechanics' Institution, the home of socialists and run, in Birmingham, by Unitarians, he read much more which said differently. The strictures of early nineteenth century revivalist Christianity seem incomprehensibly short on social compassion, but revivalists like John Angell James were men of their time, social conscience hardly having drawn breath. James was earnest in his beliefs, caring within the context of those beliefs, committed to the saving of souls which was the imperative of the time and he was emotional and loving.

Portraits show a broad faced man with wide set eyes crowned with good, moderate brows. His lips were pleasantly shaped and turned up, genially, at the corners. His nose was short and stubbed. He wore no moustache, or beard, only fashionably long side-whiskers. His whole dome seems to have been led, just, by its chin. His was the appearance of a man comfortably off, which he was. Broad chested, compact frame, build 'that of a country gentleman' one contemporary said. A picture of complacency which belied the inner man.

At the time of Holyoake's walk from Birmingham to Bristol in May 1842, James had reached his fifty-seventh year and a time in his life when he was anxious about his health. He feared the pain of disease and he anticipated death. Earlier in that year, in the privacy of his room he wrote:

> *Directions for my Spiritual Conduct*
> More time for prayer – reading – meditation.
> Cultivate more spirituality.
> Seek to have the graces of faith and trust much strengthened.
> Cheerfully trust God.
> Depend not on *secondary* sources of consolation; rest on God.
> Fear not, I am with thee.

Let him take hold of my strength.
Grace sufficient.
Able to do exceeding abundantly.
All this to oppose a distrustful state with respect to the prospect of suffering from apprehended disease.
Realise the approach of death – eternity.
Domestic
To endeavour to make the house as cheerful as possible.
To be punctual, solemn in family devotions as if many more.
To continue the practice of not supping out. [17]

Nor was the young Holyoake a stranger to ill health, physical and mental. He had left his parents' home to live independently in the summer of 1838, a few months after his first meeting with George Combe and at a time when he was still working at the Eagle Foundry, teaching mathematics at both the Unitarian Sunday school and to the Mechanics' Institution's adult attendees, and while he continued his own studies necessarily late into the night. These activities brought on a nervous collapse. The perceptive doctor who was consulted recommended a walking holiday as a restorative.

Holyoake set off on what was the first of many walks he made through the country. 'Columbus' he said, 'was not more enchanted at seeing new lands than I was at seeing new places'.[18] Continuing in the slightly self-conscious prose style which marks his memoirs, he recalls:

> No bridge, no stream, no mountain, no castle, no battle-ground, no spot of historic beauty, had hitherto met my sight. Over the foundry walls where I worked had come gleams of the sun, which had made me long to see the outlying world on which it shone unconfined. Now I was in that world; happy days were those, for my heart was as light as my purse! [19]

To Ellen Williams, his fiancée, he wrote from Buxton on the 13th of September, 'Since I left you I have been to Lichfield Cathedral, tasted the famous Ale of Burton, passed through Derby, bathed in the beautiful Bath of Matlock and have just now returned from walking and bathing in the splendid Crescent of Buxton'.[20] His way also took him through Manchester, where, even this early in his career, he was known and welcomed by the Salford trades unionists, then on to Liverpool to spend 'enchanted days among ships – never having seen any before'. He took a steamer to the Isle of Man and spent a week in Douglas feeding on fishes, then, returning to the mainland via North Wales, slept one night in an inn at the foot of Snowdon. He slept a full twelve hours, a sign that his mental agitation, which had allowed him no more than six hours rest each night for many months past, was over. He passed through Bettws-y-Coed and Boscobel and everywhere he went he talked to people.

> Now I had seen the mountain where Nature keeps an outlook on her dominions, hamlets sleeping in their morning beauty, and incessant towns where nothing is still. I had seen even the bewitching peace of the sea and had been on it when it was roused... What I had seen convinced me that not even ignorance could repress the resilient diversity of humanity, and that new knowledge infinitely multiplies itself. [21]

This journey probably settled the question of John Angell James's influence upon him. Through many of the preceding months Holyoake had attended lectures on socialism given by his friends Frederick Hollick and John Hornblower. On the eleventh of February he had heard Hollick speak on 'Social Religion', a method which rejected notions of personal salvation and instead embraced the charitable view that we 'are not blameable for unbelief', nor does the socialist 'pray for blessings to alight on him or calamities to be averted from him, but he endeavours to live in accordance with the Laws of his nature'. [22]

Perhaps with the deliberate intention to compare the two, Holyoake three days later attended a sermon given by John Angell James on Infidelity. He came away feeling that to expect God's support in return for believing in the Word was a presumption and that the notion of a God who condemns unbelievers to damnation was morally indefensible. If, as James said, the infidel dashes with one fell hand Christ's cup of hope from the inhabitants of one thousand dreary homes, 'why', Holyoake began to ask himself, 'is the cup of hope wanted, why *are* there dreary homes in want of light?' The answer seemed plain enough. When it came to improving the lives of working families, 'Christianity is impotent or has been'.[23]

Holyoake turned to Socialism and did not enter Carrs Lane Chapel again for many years.

3

A solar eclipse occurred on the 15th of May, 1836. George Jacob Holyoake's notebook tells us that he watched the event from Camp Hill in Birmingham. In these days he still considered himself a Christian and says he was thinking seriously about religion.[1] Nineteen years old in 1836, he wrote his thoughts on religion and man:

> Reverence for man, simply as man, for the mighty capacities of his intellect and the universal range of those affections of his which stretch through eternity, is the very root and central principle of Christianity... This principle it is which will ultimately put down slavery and war; and remove or minimize human ignorance, misery, and degradation of every kind. [2]

In his mind was the ignorance, misery and degradation of the working classes and he dreamed of the restoration of their pre-industrial independence. Throughout his teenage years he believed that Christianity was the medium through which such dreams would triumph. Christian principles and authority would raise mankind above war, slavery and everything else evil and cruel.

In 1836, while the young Holyoake concerned himself with these thoughts, John Angell James was enjoying the success of his book *The Anxious Enquirer After Salvation* which sold in impressive numbers in Britain and abroad. Certainly Holyoake read it. In all likelihood he was handed a copy by its author. Also speaking from the heart, James sought to bring his reader to the way of religious conversion, a 'coming to the knowledge of truth'.[3] The way was couched in apocalyptic prose, frightening to some, and tortuous in its attempt to reconcile a theology of the elect with the possibility of salvation for all. He starts at the heart of the matter:

> *You are an immortal creature, a being born for eternity, a creature that will never go out of existence.* Millions of ages, as numerous as the sands upon

> the shore, and the drops of the ocean, and the leaves of all the forests on the globe, will not shorten the duration of your being; vast eternity, incomprehensible eternity, is before you. Every day brings you nearer to everlasting torments or felicity. [4]

He continues, 'except you repent, my reader, you will perish; perish body and soul in the bottomless pit, and perish everlastingly. There is a world of misery in that word, perish; it is deep as hell, broad as infinity, and long as eternity. None can comprehend its meaning but lost souls; and they are ever discovering in it some new mystery of torment'.[5] Prose to thrill the nerves. *The Anxious Enquirer* expends all its pages on ways to personal salvation, itself depending on combinations of feeling, conviction, determination, submission and belief. The actual anxious enquirer is to spend every free moment in contemplation and pursuit of the saving of his immortal soul. If we cannot receive, or achieve, conversion through faith, our destiny will be eternal torment, and John Angell James truly dreaded the thought of one of his flock falling to this fate.

If you were a town or country labourer, the times were too hard on the body for the mind to dwell much upon the saving of the soul. For the majority, to be condemned to worse than this life after death by those who presented themselves as God's emissaries and earthly dispensers of divine judgement was a bitter harvest. In the mid-1830s, years which could be described as the last years of innocence for George Jacob Holyoake, English townships were still a growing phenomena. London's population was fewer than two million, Birmingham's not even close to a quarter of a million and all closely packed. For the industrial labourers of Birmingham's brassfounders, button-makers, milliners and shoemakers, goldsmiths and silversmiths, gunsmiths, glass blowers and dealers in iron and steel, life was not as bad as elsewhere. Children were overworked but generally laboured no more than ten hours a day; they went hungry but infant mortality was greater in Manchester and Leeds. If you lived in Birmingham you were less likely to die from typhus than in other urban areas thanks to the benefits of good natural drainage.

Beyond the town's southerly boundaries, at Bordesley to the east, Edgbaston to the west, stretched countryside in which the Devil or the land owners, depending on your view, visited much misery upon large numbers of its human inhabitants. For as long as he could keep fit, an agricultural labourer that day might earn two or three pennies for setting a bushel of beans or for digging yards of ditching; winter pay might be six shillings (30 pence in today's terms) a week plus some cider or beer. Women and children were paid pennies for a week's work in the fields. Their cottages had nothing to recommend them. Consisting of timber, plaster and thatch, they were 'merely a shelter from the weather, without any particular attention having been paid to comfort and convenience'.[6]

It was probably with a nod that Holyoake greeted those he met along the road to Worcester on that warm May morning of 1842. His allegiance might lie with the labouring people but he was always aware of his mental superiority over them. A guess at the train of his thoughts as he passed by the cottages and fields of Worcestershire might be that poverty and disaffection were the results of the withholding by the powerful of education and opportunity to the powerless; that religion kept the poor in a state of ignorant dependence for its own and the state's benefit; and that learning and self-sufficiency were the only means to working-class regeneration. Poor men, he would later write 'will find that every inch of ground, every flower of the field, every bird of the air, every spray on the sea has an owner; but there is one thing at least left him – he may be master of his own mind; his intellect at least is in his own keeping'.[7]

His views had changed a great deal from those of the obedient, religious-minded boy who had attended John Angell James's Sunday school those few years before, the boy who believed in Christianity as the answer to all social evils, and who wholeheartedly had believed that prayer was powerful enough to bring relief from suffering. Such notions were behind him and he now looked to more practical means for salvation. Earlier events as well as thought had brought him to this point. Thirteen years earlier his baby sister Eliza had died at home while their mother was kept away for too long in answer to a summons for over-due church rates. It is not clear whether or not the twelve-year-old boy was in the house with the dying child, but the horror of this event produced in him a growing dislike of the church. At a later date, when his mother returned, distraught, from Carrs Lane Chapel one Sunday night to tell her family that the Reverend James had told the congregation of sins never to be forgiven and of 'children in hell not a span long', his dislike grew into a 'silent terror of Christianity'.[8] The boy found it hard to justify all this with the idea of a religion promising to answer the prayers of those who believed; a religion which would remove 'degradation of every kind'.

During the years in which he wrestled with his doubts he abandoned John Angell James' chapel in Carrs Lane for one in Inge Street. It was not until the day that the Reverend Tully Cribbace came to Birmingham that the last of his hopes in religion were quenched. Mr. Cribbace was a 'middle-aged man with copious dark hair, pale, thin face, and earnest, unceasing speech', and who upbraided his listeners for shallow faith in the promise of prayer. Holyoake, who had arrived at a critical point in his spiritual progress, visited Mr Cribbace at his lodgings in Newhall Street after hearing him preach, to ask whether he had been in earnest when he had said that whatever we should ask would be given. He had in mind relief of the poor, for in his experience nothing mattered more.

Would prayer remove poverty? Holyoake recalls how the visiting preacher, himself in a visible state of impoverishment, 'parried with his answer with many words' but at length said that 'the promise was to be taken with the provision that what we asked for would be given, if God thought it for our good'. Holyoake, with his rational mind, felt sure Christ did not think this:

> knowing how many generations of men to the end of the world would imperil their lives on the truth of His words, He could not suffer treacherous ambiguity to creep into His meaning by omission. His words were: "If it were not so, I would have told you". There was no double meaning in Christ... My heart sank within me as Mr. Cribbace spoke the words of evasion. [9]

This sad encounter was the turning point for Holyoake. He never felt the same about his religion after this conversation with Mr Cribbace who, inadvertently, had dealt the fatal blow which would bring an end to a young man's Christian faith. Holyoake had been assured the Bible was a divine revelation, the literal word of a God on which man could depend. But 'is not the sense of dependence outraged already?' he later put it, when 'man witnesses those near and dear to him perish before his eyes... despite his supplications. He walks through no rose-water world, and no special Providence smoothes his path'.[10]

Holyoake's thoughts were as much embedded in absolutes as those of his religious mentors', his in reason and logic, the churches' in doctrine and faith. It is hardly surprising that the source of religious faith should fail a young man with such a logical turn of mind, especially when his family and friends suffered through a lack of life's necessities while ministers of the church appeared to do little more than talk of human depravity and personal salvation. Moral revulsion at this propelled Holyoake away from the theology of these men, he began to look elsewhere for deliverance from the social evils of the day. He remained a deist while his faith in Christianity fell away. Political socialism was a natural next step as it was the only organised form of expression open to anyone of Holyoake's stamp.

As early as 1832, when just fifteen years old, he had joined the Birmingham Political Union, a parliamentary reform group which later supported the aims of the Chartist movement. Holyoake joined the Union in the aftermath of the passing of the Great Reform Act of that year which was a triumph for the rising classes but a crushing blow to the mass of working men, for the Act had succeeded in keeping the vote from them. All women were denied the franchise. On top of this, these were years of poor harvests, bread selling at inflated prices due to the Corn Laws*, bad trading conditions and controversial legislation to regulate relief of the destitute. All these had deepened the difficulties and alienation of working families who remained powerless to improve their lot.

For the remainder of his teenage years, the metal of Holyoake's social and religious radicalism was forged in the company of Unitarian and socialist friends at Birmingham's Mechanics' Institution, housed in the Unitarian's Old Meeting-house which was, in fact, a new building, the earlier one on Worcester Street having been razed to the ground during the Priestley riots of 1791. It was here that he met William Hawkes Smith and Daniel Wright, tutors at the Institution, and fellow students Frederick Hollick and John Hornblower who would become Holyoake's brother-in-law. Recollections of his early association with this group, which began when he was about sixteen years old, shows how unswervingly literal his thinking was. Asked by one of his fellows what were his views regarding the Deity, he replied that he believed in three Deities: Father, Son and Holy Ghost. He did, however, grow to appreciate the Unitarian principle which 'trusts God and never fears him' and which is 'the instinct of civilization'.[11]

By no means did he fall into the arms of the Unitarians as if delivered from error. His reaction to this group mirrors John Angell James's to the mimic play he had attended at much the same age. When Holyoake agreed to teach mathematics and the elements of logic to the Unitarian's Sunday School pupils, he would sit after lessons with his charges in the chapel and as near to the stairs (and exit) as possible, just in case the wickedness of the preacher, who believed in one Deity, brought the wrath of God, and the ceiling, down upon their heads.

Holyoake joined another political society in 1838 which met at No. 6 Church Street, Birmingham, the address of a Mr. Jenkinson, bookseller. 'It

* Imposed in 1815, the Corn Laws allowed duty to be applied to imported corn if the price of home produced wheat did not reach 80 shillings per quarter. This boosted the profits of landowners whilst maintaining a protected high purchase price for bread. The Anti-Corn Law League saw their cause as a struggle between the poor who subsisted on bread, and the land-owning corn producers who, even after 1832, held two-thirds of the seats in the House of Commons. The Corn Laws were not repealed until 1846.

proved to be a Foreign Affairs Committee,' Holyoake recalls, 'The object to be to cut off Lord Palmerston's head. Things were bad among workmen in those days, and I had no doubt somebody's head ought to be cut off; I hoped they had hit upon the right one'.[12] These events were to be the last of Holyoake's harmless political adventuring. Within a few months social agitation in Britain's manufacturing districts was to become the great concern in the land.

There was one last event of youthful enthusiasm for Holyoake before politics and married life took him from theory to action. He ended that pivotal year of 1838 with three consecutive nights on the roof of the Eagle Foundry counting comets. For this purpose Birmingham's Philosophical Society provided Holyoake and two companions with 'a thermometer, an electrometer and a magnetic needle' together with instructions to 'register the appearance of every meteor and to look for manifestations of the Aurora'.

The number of meteors observed during the three nights was one hundred and fifty-four and Holyoake wrote that 'The rocket that was seen at 10' past 12 [Monday, twelfth November] was the most beautiful we saw during any of the nights, its luminous train, which remained visible some seconds, extended nearly from Horizon to Horizon'. The Aurora Borealis appeared on the next night, the thirteenth, 'when the appearance of the horizon was gloomy, a sheet of very faint grey light shot up in the North and North West. At 5' to 2 it became stronger and extended towards the North East. At 2 o'clock it was much more vivid. At 5' past 2 faint streaks of white light began to strike up to about 15 degrees of Altitude, in the North West. At 15' past 2 two more streaks of crimson and red shot up in the North West by West to about 45 degrees of Altitude. At 30' past 2 the two streaks in the North East by North became glaringly red, coming again until 4 a.m. At 5 o'clock it again appeared, the central streaks reaching to about 60 degrees of Altitude, the upper parts tinged with crimson... The whole vanished at 5 past 5'. [13]

A symbolic vanishing in some ways, a vanishing of youthfulness and celestial hopes, for by now Holyoake was definitely looking not to churches but to practical social reform for working class deliverance from poverty and humiliation. Salvation and religion no longer correlated in his brain. In this year of 1838 he had been so busy meeting George Combe, counting comets, teaching, journeying to the Isle of Man and back, and courting his wife-to-be Ellen Williams, that a Chartist revival which, after the disappointment of 1832, was taking place in Birmingham, must have taken a back seat to these activities. In fact, this revival was to presage events that would propel the young

Holyoake into his adult years as a spirited radical, determined to change the status quo. The Chartist Bull Ring riot of the following year was a disaster biding its time and, for Holyoake, would come as a rude shock, a dark, dismal contrast to the pleasures he had experienced during his happy perambulation six months earlier.

4

The Chartists called for a vote for every man. They wanted annual parliaments, private vote by ballot, abolition of the property qualification, payment for MPs and reform of electoral districts – through which many densely populated urban areas would be granted Parliamentary representation. 'What they wanted', Benjamin Wilson wrote, 'was a voice in making the laws they were called upon to obey; they believed that taxation without representation was tyranny, and ought to be resisted, they took a leading part in agitating in favour of the ten hours question, the repeal of the taxes on knowledge, education, co-operation, civil and religious liberty, and the land question, for they were the true pioneers in all the great movements of the time'.[1]

The 1839 Charter was a scroll inscribed with more than a million signatures. A huge document in physical terms, it was carried into the House of Commons on the 14th of June and presented to its members by Thomas Attwood, Liberal member for Birmingham and driving force behind the reformist Birmingham Political Union. As the petition was brought up it produced loud laughter from its gigantic dimensions and Attwood 'unrolled a sufficient portion of it to enable him to place one extremity of it on the clerk's table'. Turning to the assembly, Mr Attwood said:

> There has been one universal anxious cry of distress... long disregarded by this House... which has caused much discontent amongst the working people, and which discontent is created by the long sufferings and grievances which that class of the people has endured. At all the meetings which have been held, the persons attending them have confined themselves strictly to the legal pursuit of their constitutional rights... They met with no support, or even sympathy, from this House, and, therefore, they feel themselves bound to exercise every legal and constitutional effort within their power to recover the whole of their constitutional rights. [2]

Throughout the spring of 1839 meetings and parades of angry Chartists had been held daily in the streets of Birmingham, and when parliament formerly rejected the Charter in July, physical force Chartism, advocated for months past by the movement's leader, Feargus O'Connor, flamed in followers' hearts where before it had simmered. 'Despair', Holyoake recalls 'was diffused like a pestilence'. Then a young man of twenty-two years and by nature much too reasonable and respectable to participate in violent protest, he watched the consequences unfold in Birmingham. 'The prospects of the working class' he wrote, 'could not be worse':

> Not the ignorant alone, but educated men, then and since, were of the same way of thinking, and said so... Hundreds made arms secretly. Those who had no better weapons sharpened an old file and stuck it in a haft. I saw many such. A dozen gentlemen in the town, who had sympathy with the just discontent of the people, could have kept the peace with applause. [3]

Birmingham had received its Charter of Incorporation the year before and its magistrates were unschooled in the art of public order. A troop of Dragoons was recruited to keep peace in the town and then a contingent of police was sent for from London by, according to Holyoake, these 'sapient and contemptuous magistrates'. It was this last act which, according to some, was the cause of what was to come. The Londoners arrived by rail at Birmingham with 'orders to break up the meetings and arrest the leaders'.[4] They promptly attacked, and successfully scattered, the crowd which had gathered in the Bull Ring until, according to an eye witness, the people rallied and surrounded them. 'Some [police] were knocked down, some kicked, some stabbed and stoned; and had it not been for the arrival of the military the entire of them would have fallen a sacrifice to the fury of the people'.[5]

After watching London policemen attack his Birmingham neighbours, Holyoake was to wonder 'what Irishmen must think of having their heads broken by alien ruffians of order, sent over from England, when Birmingham men treated London policemen as aliens'.[6] After this, mayor and magistrate, with breath held, prepared for the worst.

On Monday, the fifteenth of July, Chartist leaders William Lovett and John Collins, arrested for publishing a placard in support of the public action that was taking place, were taken to Birmingham's Public Office where a panel of magistrates committed them to trial at Warwick. A crowd had gathered in Moor Street and dispersed quietly enough upon learning the results of the hearing. The soldiers sat in their barracks, the police in their quarters, the mayor went to dinner, the magistrates went home. None was especially concerned when an evening crowd, peaceable it seems, began to gather in the Bull Ring. It was at about eight o'clock when, according to contemporary reports, a marching band of armed men came up Digbeth, turned down Moor Street and began their business with a violent assault upon the Public Office before proceeding to the Bull Ring, demolishing shop windows as they went. "Remember it?" reiterated one shop manager when asked:

> About eight o'clock, amid increasing uproar in the street, there came a cry of 'Fire', and on proceeding to an upper floor I saw the glare of fire reflected in the windows of the opposite house. I at once collected all the assistants and porters, and proceeding to the shop, we alighted the gas and mustered all the 'arms' in the house. They consisted of an old sword and a horse pistol, the latter of which we loaded with ball. The front door was a very wide one, and here I planted one of the porters with a large kitchen poker. In one of the windows I placed a strong man with a crowbar, and in the other an active fellow with the sword. Presently we heard our upper windows smashing, and simultaneously, an attack was made upon our front door and windows by men armed with railings they had taken from Nelson's monument... I, myself, knocked one fellow senseless by a blow from a four-pound weight which I dashed full in his face.
>
> ... All at once there was a cry, a roar, and a sound of horses' hoofs. A moment afterwards we saw a troop of Dragoons come tearing along, with swords drawn, slashing away on all sides. Some of the rioters were very badly cut, and the affrighted ruffians fled in all directions, amid groans, cries, curses, and a horrid turmoil. [7]

Holyoake was there for the whole of it, 'if not an actor a sympathizer'. 'Some frenzied men set fire to houses in revenge' he recalls,

> Soldiers were brought out, and a neighbour of mine, who happened to be standing unarmed and looking on at the corner of Edgbaston Street, had his nose chopped off... At four o'clock next morning I went with my wife, who wished to see whether Mr. Belcher, whose house had been fired, needed aid in his household, as she had great respect for him. Although we alone crossed the Bull Ring, the soldiers rushed at us, and tried to cut me down. I did not like them. Until then I thought the duty of a policeman

> or soldier was to keep his head, protect the people, and keep the peace except in self-defence. [8]

This was Holyoake's first experience of state violence. 'Soldiers, like policemen, soon know when outrages are expected of them', he wrote. His hatred of magistrates, that unenviable group administratively squashed between the under- and the upper-classes, and who rarely pleased either, would intensify from this time on.

On the day following the Monday riot the atmosphere in Birmingham was repressive. Dragoons and riflemen were strategically positioned throughout the town, policemen patrolled the streets. On that morning, as Holyoake and his wife, who by this time was expecting their first child, walked across the Bull Ring, they would have seen the 'medley of miscellaneous items', the remains of destruction strewn across the place and the half-burnt arm chair in which some of the police specials, as a symbol of their victory, had placed a large, circular tea-canister, 'in imitation of a sitting figure... which, in its battered condition, bore some rough resemblance to a human form'.[9] This tea-canister had been given clothing, a hat and a pipe stuck into a hole where a mouth should be.

* * * * *

Now, almost three years on from these events and as he walked through the small town of Bromsgrove and on to Droitwich, Holyoake would be acutely aware of parliament's rejection of a second People's Charter two weeks earlier. This largest of all the Chartist petitions was a scroll so huge that the shoulders of sixteen men were barely enough to carry it through the streets of London to Westminster and which, in a sense tragically, had to be broken up before it could pass through the doorway to the Chamber. The House received it with laughter and rejected it by a big majority. Thomas Slingsby Duncombe, Member for Finsbury, who presented the petition to the House, promised that this was the last time he would take on any proposition of this kind after seeing the manner in which the petitioners were treated.

All, again, had resulted in disappointment for the Chartists, the depths of which it is hard to imagine but which would not discourage their leaders from supporting the general strike which would engulf the northern counties and southern Scotland over the summer months of 1842. Holyoake was not active in the Chartist movement, but was outraged by the attitude of the ruling classes. Had it been in his nature, he might have thought to stop off at the brine pits at Droitwich to rub a handful or two of salt into the wounds.

By this stage in his journey, George Jacob Holyoake had grown to be an angry young man. He was angered by the reaction of church and magistrate against free-thought and expression, by parliament and its denial of working men's rights, and now he was deeply disappointed in a hope he had harboured for the relief of the working-classes. This hope had been gendered by the utopian socialist movement of Robert Owen, an alternative to practical and political Chartism, which Holyoake had been actively promoting for the past three years.

5

The socialist movement of the early 1800s was the work of Robert Owen, a man whom George Jacob Holyoake first heard speak on the 15th of June, 1836, at the Allison Street Rooms, Birmingham. Then still a practicing Christian, Holyoake went along with John Hornblower* and other friends, thinking he was going to hear the Reverend Robert Hall whom he admired. Robert Hall had died in 1831 but the young Holyoake, not knowing this, thought he was to hear an address from the preacher who stood for universal suffrage, a free press and Church disestablishment, and who believed that love should prevail in the hearts of Christians. Robert Hall differed from Robert Owen in believing that morality without faith is of 'no avail in the eye of God', so Holyoake was in for an interesting evening. He had scarcely heard of Owen and was greatly disappointed when he realised his mistake. It seems he knew enough about him to think him a 'wicked old man'. Owen was by now in his sixties and on entering the room, and as he passed Holyoake, the young philosopher's eyes fell upon him for the first time and he felt pity and some contempt for the man who would, before long, become a significant influence on him for years to come.

Robert Owen was a man of blithe spirit and uncommon vision. A man comfortable working in a capitalist system, he did, with ease, combine a natural entrepreneurial ability with a care, unusual for the day, for the welfare of his workers. He inspired many to believe in a New Moral World. He made heavy investment with his own, and others' money in pursuit of it. His memoirs are full of happy allusions to his being 'a favourite' of a great many of those who knew him. If he was not a favourite, then it was not his fault. A happy man who, William Hazlitt said, had but one idea, but what an idea: to make this land 'a fit abode for superior men and women, under a New

---

* later reports say it was Frederick Hollick who took Holyoake to the meeting, but Holyoake's Log Book suggests it was Hornblower.

Dispensation, which will make the earth a paradise and its inhabitants angels'.[1] Self-assurance and optimism ran through his veins as surely as, in those days, moral pessimism flowed in the blood of religious orthodoxy from which he took it upon himself to free us all. Robert Owen spent his life pursuing a utopian dream where every man and woman would live freely and happily, well fed and spiritually fulfilled.

The son of a saddle-maker who also functioned as the local postmaster at Newtown in Montgomeryshire, Owen was taught reading, writing and arithmetic as a boy, the rest of his education he pursued independently. In 1780, when he was just nine years old, he decided that life in his home town was too dull and he asked his parents' permission to leave home so that he could live in London with his elder brother William, already married:

> Having by this period read much of other countries and other proceedings, and, with my habits of reflection and extreme temperance, not liking the habits and manners of a small country town, I began to desire a different field of action, and wished my parents to permit me to go to London. I was at this time about nine years and a half old; and at length, although I was a great favourite at home, it was promised that when I should attain my tenth year I should be allowed to go. [2]

He left, it seems, without a backward glance. He was a remarkably independently spirited young man, and this, combined with a mental agility and willingness to jump in feet first, took him in less than ten years from shop boy in a retail haberdasher's shop at £8 a year, to manager of one of Britain's first and greatest cotton spinning mills on a salary of £300 per annum, and then his career was only just begun.

It was during his four years with his first employer, Mr McGuffog of Stamford, Lincolnshire, that Owen, still a boy, began to think critically about religion. Mr. McGuffog was of the Church of Scotland, his wife of the Church of England, and their apprentice would accompany each to their church of preference, one in the morning, the other in the afternoon of every Sunday. 'I was all this time endeavouring to find out *the true religion*', recalls Owen:

> and was greatly puzzled for some time by finding all of every sect over the world, of which I read, or of which I heard from the pulpits, claim each for themselves to be in possession of *the true religion*. I studied, and studied, and carefully compared one with another, for I was very religiously

> inclined, and desired most anxiously to be in the right way. But the more I heard, read, and reflected, the more I became dissatisfied with Christian, Jew, Mahomedan, Hindoo, Chinese, and Pagan. [3]

After four happy years with the McGuffogs, Owen again grew restless: 'my wishes were for the attainment of more knowledge and an enlarged field of action'. He returned to London, saw the sights and walked the parks with his brother and sister-in-law, then took up employment with Messrs Flint and Palmer 'an old established house on old London Bridge, Borough side, overlooking the Thames'. This was the London which existed before the enthusiasm of early nineteenth century developers changed it beyond recall, vestiges of which Dickens would know and George Holyoake fall in love with. It was a London where haberdashers' assistants sometimes worked from eight in the morning until two the following morning, and where each, at Messrs Flint and Palmer at any rate, had to wait their turn for the hairdresser each morning to 'powder and pomatum and curl' their hair. Robert Owen, a fifteen year old who then spoke in an ungrammatical 'kind of Welsh English', had two large curls on each side of his head 'and a stiff pigtail, and until this was very nicely and systematically done, no one could think of appearing before a customer'. [4]

The working conditions under which he and his fellow shop assistants laboured was a point of interest to him, but not a rule by which he would be subsumed. By the time he was eighteen he had left London. He was now in Manchester and about to borrow his first £100 from his brother William to start a business making machines for spinning cotton. Owen had absolutely no knowledge of the cotton industry beyond the stuff he had sold over the counter, but he was in the right place at the right time. He and his partner Jones ('a mere mechanic' Owen later called him and whom Owen had met behind Mr Satterfield's haberdasher's counter, located in a shop in St. Annes Square), obtained 'wood, iron, and brass, for their construction upon credit'. By 1791, in a warehouse near the New Bridge, Dolefield (now Bridge Street) they began their manufacture of mule machines and roving frames. The business partnership foundered within a year and Owen advanced on his own with three mule machines, all he had left to show of his partnership with Jones the mechanic, and three men to work them, 'that is' he said:

> to spin cotton yarn or thread upon them from a previous preparation called rovings. When the yarn was spun, it was in the cup form, from which it was

> to be made upon the reel into hanks, each one hundred and forty yards in length. This operation I performed, and then made these hanks into bundles of five pounds weight each, and in this state wrapped neatly up in paper. I sold them to a Mr Mitchell, an agent from some mercantile manufacturing houses in Glasgow, who sold the yarn to muslin weavers, or manufactured it themselves. [5]

From these beginnings Owen progressed to the employ of Peter Drinkwater, owner of Manchester's great cotton spinning mill at Bank Top. Drinkwater, in an inspired moment, agreed to employ the untried nineteen-year-old Owen as his mill manager. Also known as the Piccadilly Factory, Bank Top was an impressive and innovative building. Peter Drinkwater not only had acquired a rotary steam engine to power the place, a first in the industry, from Boulton and Watt's Soho Works in Birmingham, he also had installed lavatories for his workers with stench trap and flushing water 'let out from the great wooden cistern of the engine'.[6]

The mill lay just off the London Road in Manchester, between Auburn Street and Upton Street, and it was filled with mules of one hundred and forty-four spindles, all worked by men's hands. Of its five hundred work people and machinery Owen knew very little, and as he entered the mill he experienced an unfamiliar self doubt and real fear that he could not cope with so huge a responsibility. His feeling for human nature was such that he based his approach to worker relations on a mutual respect between himself and his employees which he did not complicate with any sense of sentimentality and, abetted by Peter Drinkwater's enlightened attitude to working conditions, Owen saw that his system worked. Under his management, quality of production and profit at Bank Top mill increased substantially.

Owen stayed at Bank Top until 1794 and his memoirs move from mention of his being 'but an ill-educated awkward youth, strongly sensitive' to easy talk of 'my Manchester partners' as smoothly and swiftly as butter, flour and milk turn to béchamel sauce. His transition from enterprising youth to established business man with aristocratic tastes ran upon oiled bearings and by the time he and his partners bought New Lanark mills from his father-in-law, David Dale, in 1799, his future and principles were set.

> I had by this period perceived the constant influence of circumstances over my own proceedings and those of others, and... [r]elieved from religious prejudices and their obstructive influence... I was obliged to consider my

> fellow men as being made of circumstances before and after their birth, not under their own control... and therefore to have illimitable charity for their feelings, thoughts and actions. My mind, in consequence, gradually became calm and serene, and anger and ill-will died within me. [7]

Improve conditions for the working people, he began to tell his friends and fellow capitalists, and nobility of character will grow even in the poorest human specimen. 'When I mentioned' he recalls, 'that my intention was to commence a new system of [factory] management, on principles of justice and kindness... they one and all smiled at my simplicity in imagining I could succeed in such a visionary scheme, and strongly urged me not to attempt so hopeless a task'.[8] His was not a new idea, but Owen brought to it a determination to act upon it. He invested his own and his partners' money in a social experiment at the mills at New Lanark, the genesis of the New Moral World.

Small wooden monitors were hung by each mill worker which told, through colour coding, the conduct of the individual. Personal hygiene was advanced, exemplary sexual conduct expected, theft was eradicated through rigorous stock-taking. All religious predilections were tolerated, dancing encouraged, evening classes proliferated and, for the children, schooling. No child was to work in the mills before the age of ten and 'whatever may be said to the contrary,' Owen later wrote,

> bad and unwise as American slavery is and must continue to be, the white slavery in the manufactories of England was at this unrestricted period far worse than the house slaves whom I afterwards saw in the West Indies and in the United States, and in many respects, especially as regards health, food, and clothing, the latter were much better provided for than were these oppressed and degraded children and workpeople in the home manufactories of Great Britain. [9]

Lloyd Jones, one of Owen's later associates, had something to say about the system of early factory employment of children: 'the plan was to obtain as apprentices, from the various workhouses of the kingdom, as large a number of the pauper children as were required, and bind them under indenture... They were bargained for and sent to their destination in droves; the workhouse authorities, glad enough to get rid of them, prudently stipulating that those who contracted for them should take a due proportion of the ailing and idiotic. When these children entered on the employment at which they were to spend their lives, they were housed and bedded in sheds; their food was of the poorest kind... These poor creatures were unable to look after themselves, and, as there was no one near connected with them by ties of blood, they were entirely at the mercy of those who regarded them solely as implements of labour. The records we possess of the treatment and suffering of these children are heartrending' [10]

Through the system he established at New Lanark, Owen manipulated his workers' behaviour to the benefit of themselves and of mill production. The place was a wonder of its time which many influential visitors came to experience. For Owen, this was just the start. The mill and its community were the prototype of the great and rejuvenated British society which lay ahead, next would be reformation of the world. One great obstacle stood in the way of the creation of the New Moral World, and that was the effects on society of the imposition of the moral codes preached by the world's established religions. 'The Religions founded under the name of Jewish, Budh, Jehovah, God or Christ, Mahomet or any other... amount only to three absurdities', wrote Owen:

> The fundamental doctrines or laws of all these religions are, first, – *Believe in my doctrines, as expounded by my Priests, from my sacred books*; second, *Feel as these doctrines, thus expounded, direct you to feel*; and third, *Support my Ministers for thus instructing you.* "If you faithfully perform these three things in my name." – say the Priests of all these religions – "you will have the greatest merit in this world, and an everlasting reward in the next." [11]

The gulf between Owen's and the church's philosophy was deep and wide. The churches saw human nature as sinful and which could only be reformed through faith in Christ as expounded by the church. Owen's philosophy was based on his belief in human goodness and that no man could expect to change his nature but that character should be formed properly, through corrective social engineering. The writings and sermons of John Angell James are the perfect antithesis to Owen's philosophy in their convoluted construct towards personal salvation, based on the belief that man must seek a change in his nature. James's *The Anxious Inquirer* is one man's earnest attempt to convince others to believe as he does, and it is a belief which emphasises the sinfulness of our nature, as well as that of our acts: 'the heart is a polluted fountain from whence all the muddy streams of evil conduct flow'[12] wrote James. In contrast to this, Owen saw us as creatures of spiritual beauty, the germ of which is produced by an Incomprehensible Power. 'It is' he wrote, 'therefore...':

> rank impiety and blasphemy... to say that man, at his birth, the immediate and most wonderful known work of that Incomprehensible Power, is bad or defective by nature. [13]

In March of that tumultuous year, 1817, Robert Owen presented a Report to a House of Commons Committee considering the Poor Laws, in which he laid out his social plans which were founded on the development of villages where the poor would live and where, through architectural planning and social engineering, the very best in human nature would grow so that all human necessity to exercise greed and uncharitable behaviour would be eradicated. His views were well received but he had as yet made no criticism of religion. A conviction, though, was growing in him that a day would come when he must.

Five months later, on the twenty-first day of August, 1817, he held the second of two public meetings at the City of London Tavern where he 'emphatically and solemnly, at the risk of all that men hold dear... denounced in the strongest terms all the religions as they were taught to the world'. His own account is best:

> Intending to pave the way to supersede the present false and wicked system, as I had discovered it to be, by the true and good system for governing the human race and new-forming the character of all humanity, I knew it was useless to wage a little or a covert war against a system established through the proceedings of all past times in the minds and habits of the present generation, and that ultimate success could be anticipated only from an open front attack...
>
> I knew well that the man who should have the temerity to openly denounce this system of thick mental darkness, must anticipate the opposition of that power, by and through all its darkest means of acting. My mind, however, was made up for the contest, whatever might be its consequences.
>
> When I went to this meeting, ever-to-be remembered in the annals of history, no one except myself had any notion of what I intended to do and to say... The then friends of my views, so far as I had disclosed them, came in continually increasing numbers, – the great majority of these being of the best disposed among the upper classes in church and state, and of the upper portion of the middle classes, who were sincerely desirous to improve the condition of the poor and working classes, if it could be done in order, in peace, and without a revolution of violence... .

This meeting was densely crowded, although held at noon, and again hundreds and thousands had to be disappointed who could not gain admittance, and many waited until five o'clock before any moved to allow of their entrance, and even afterwards, until its dismissal at seven, it remained crowded... Knowing what I intended to do, I went alone, that no one might be implicated in my proceedings. When I went to this meeting I was on the morning of that day by far the most popular individual in the civilised world, and possessed the most influence with a majority of the leading members of the British cabinet and government. I went to the meeting with the determination by one sentence to destroy that popularity, but by its destruction to lay the axe to the root of all false religions, and thus to prepare the population of the world for the reign of charity in accordance with the natural laws of humanity...

I commenced my address, and continued amidst much applause and cheering from the friends of the cause which I advocated, until I approached that part in which I denounced all the religions of the world as now taught; when by my manner I prepared the audience for some extraordinary proceeding. And when in a firm voice I said – "A more important question has never been put to the sons of men – who can answer it? Who dares answer it? but with his life in his hand – a ready and willing victim to truth, and to the emancipation of the world from its long bondage of error, crime, and misery? Behold that victim! On this day! in this hour! even now! shall those bonds be burst asunder, never more to re-unite while the world lasts! what the consequences of this daring deed shall be to myself I am as indifferent about, as whether it shall rain or be fair to-morrow! whatever may be the consequences, I will now perform my duty to you and to the world. And should it be the last act of my life, I shall be well content, and shall know that I have lived for an important purpose. Then, my friends! I tell you, that hitherto you have been prevented from knowing what happiness really is, solely in consequence of the errors – gross errors – " The meeting here became excited to the highest pitch of expectation as to what was to follow; and a breathless silence prevailed, so that not the slightest sound could be heard. I made a slight pause, and, as my friend afterward told me, added a great increase of strength of feeling and dignity to my manner, of which at the time I was wholly unconscious, and in that state of mind I finished the sentence – "gross errors – that have been combined with the fundamental notions of every religion that has hitherto been taught to men, And, in consequence, they have made man

> the most inconsistent, and the most miserable being in existence. By the errors of these systems he has been made a weak, imbecile animal; a furious bigot and fanatic; or a miserable hypocrite; and should these qualities be carried, not only into the projected villages, but *into Paradise itself, a Paradise would be no longer found!*" [14]

This speech was an act of professional suicide at a time when his influence was at its greatest. The room fell into a profound silence, some clerics hissed, then there was the sudden applause of friends desperate to salvage something of Owen's dignity in the face of disaster. Jacob Bright, brother of John, described Owen as 'really reckless of his own fame... no leader ever took so little care in guarding his own reputation'. Owen rode the storm well enough, the social cause went forward but was 'condemned' Jacob Bright wrote, '... ever after to the hands of the minority'. [15]

6

Owen's reputation was so great that he never was in danger of prosecution following the 1817 speech against all religions. Less well placed men would have been arrested, indicted and probably imprisoned. Instead of this, Owen went on to work towards his dream for a reformed and rational world. The Lanarkshire enterprise, in which Jeremy Bentham invested, attracted a multitude of influential visitors. Lord Brougham, who did much to promote adult education in these years, stood by Owen throughout their respective long careers, and in 1819 Edward, Duke of Kent, father of the baby girl who would become Queen Victoria, chaired Owen's meetings and publicly supported his views. He had agreed to visit Owen at Braxfield, and would have brought with him his wife and daughter, Victoria, had he lived to fulfil the engagement. Robert Owen lost an incalculably valuable supporter when Edward died in 1820.

However, the controversy over his stand on religion was to dog Owen ever after. One business partner, the Quaker William Allen, developed a 'deep exercise of mind on account of Robert Owen's infidel principles'.[1] The good results of Owen's innovative system of education for the children of Lanark, which produced surprise and fascination in visitors, was not, according to Allen, sufficiently embedded in Christian values. In 1822 he wrote to Owen saying:

> Sorry indeed am I to see that our principles are diametrically opposite; and may that Great and Holy Being, who seeth not as man sees, so influence thy heart, before the shadows of the evening close upon thee, that it may become softened and receive those impressions which He alone can give; then thou wilt perceive that there is indeed something infinitely beyond human reason, and which human reason alone can never comprehend, though in itself perfectly reasonable. *At present*, however, it is quite plain to me that *we must part.* [2]

Owen continued in good health and travelled a great deal, but failure and unfulfilled ambition were to be significant characteristics of his life from this time onwards. In the summer of 1824 he and his wife received as a guest one Richard Flower, a visitor from America and emissary from the remarkable George Rapp who had founded a successful model village on the American frontier. Rapp called his township Harmony and he ruled it as a despot. In 1814 he had moved the whole community from Butler County, Pennsylvania, to a site on the Wabash, Indiana. His followers, the inhabitants of Harmony, duly dismantled then reassembled their lives without a murmur. Owen seems never to have fathomed the fact that Rapp's remarkable success was due to his rigid, religion-centred control of everything that occurred at Harmony and his followers' willingness to pull twice their weight without question.

Now Father Rapp was on the move again, and Richard Flower was at Braxfield to see if Mr. Owen might be interested in purchasing the soon to be vacated Indiana town. Owen was an instant enthusiast, perhaps because he needed a scheme, and perhaps because a few weeks earlier another American visitor, the distinguished geologist William McClure, had unwittingly sown the New World seed in Owen's imagination when he had visited the family at Braxfield. Within three months Owen was crossing the Atlantic.

On the briefest of inspections he bought Harmony in the January of 1825, then set out back east, leaving his son William temporarily in charge of things. Owen was not thinking but dreaming, and he paid dear for the pleasure for he would lose four-fifths of his entire fortune on this ideal community, which he renamed New Harmony.

New Harmony was to be an exemplary communitarian society, but Owen's grasp on events was not as it had been in his Manchester years at Drinkwater's mill and at New Lanark, and he was dealing with different people in a very different place. These men and women were not British workers but pioneering émigrés, many of whom were island hopping from one convenient spot to another. New Harmony disintegrated into an anarchic confusion of undisciplined individuals by whom nothing got done. It also was the catalyst which brought about the disintegration of Owen's family life. His sons followed him to the New World while their mother, Caroline, was left behind in Scotland, never to see them again.[3]

After three years Owen left New Harmony to return to England, and not so many years after that his wife who, upon meeting him had declared that if she were not to marry Robert Owen she would marry no one, was dead.

After the triumphs and disappointments of the 1832 Reform Act, Owen, now back in England, saw the need for a leader for the organising working classes. He formed the Grand National Consolidated Trades Union with the intention of encouraging workers to combine in their respective crafts and industries with a pledge to strike for an eight-hour day. Sheffield trades unionist and poet, Ebenezer Elliot, said of Owen in 1834: 'You came among us as a rich man among the poor, and did not call us a rabble. This is a phenomenon new to us'.[4] Owen was riding on the slipstream of past glories and the Union, like so much else he pursued during these years, was soon dissolved. Later came the Association of All Classes of All Nations which, in 1839, transmogrified into the Universal Community Society of Rational Religionists, by which time Owen was referring to his socialist movement as a new religion.

When in 1838 George Jacob Holyoake, encouraged by Frederick Hollick, joined the Association of All Classes of All Nations as it then was, the organization supported dozens of town and city branches, each sending a delegate to an annual national congress, presided over by a Central Board, itself controlled by Robert Owen. The Chartist Movement and Owen's socialist organization were the two great hopes for those excluded from the Reform Act if their kind was to regain the dignity and independence it had enjoyed before the effects of industrialization had taken these away. Men like Holyoake dreamed of social regeneration while Owen dreamed up a system which promised to replace individualistic, commercial competition with socialistic co-operation. His focus was always on colonies which would function outside mainstream society, communitarian groups, especially formed and managed. The wealth produced by these communitarian cooperatives would be fairly redistributed – a New Moral Economy to complete The New Moral World.

The social question was deeply entangled in the religious. It is calculated that in the 1830s more than a quarter of the Justices of the Peace were clergymen; organized religion represented a repressive force to a great many working people.[5] The church upheld, in thought and deed, the social division of rich and poor, law-givers and receivers, the powerful and powerless. Some of its clergy were aware of the effects of this. W.F. Hook, vicar of Leeds, writing to Samuel Wilberforce in 1843 said that the Church 'is detested in the cities by the working classes because they consider the Church to belong to the party of their oppressors'.[6] In 1838, one of the Tolpuddle Martyrs, labourer and Methodist preacher George Loveless, had expressed his feelings for the Church of England as 'of the blackest description; we behold things which make our hearts throb with indignation'.[7] The Owenite's Birmingham branch distributed half a million anti-religious tracts in that year and, being a party to activities of this kind, this worked against Holyoake. His fellow workers at the Eagle Foundry already viewed him with suspicion. 'That's young Holyoake the sceptic' one was overheard to say. 'Sceptic' meant something more than religious doubter, it implied infidel, free-thinker, outsider. Holyoake was unaccountably affronted by this. The impression was not improved when he sold to a fellow worker his Bible, an article which, as Holyoake liked lovely things, he had had bound in morocco, with silver clasps.

When he chose to give up smithying at the Eagle Foundry to take up full-time teaching, he encountered difficulties. Due to the untimely death of Daniel Wright, the post of permanent tutor at the Mechanics' Institution fell vacant and, thinking he had 'nothing to hope, to fear, nor lose' in applying for the job, having, as he says, 'toiled, with thousands of others, who were never remunerated by the means for paltriest comfort, and whose lives were never enlivened by real pleasure', Holyoake chose to give up his trade in favour of the teaching profession.[8] He had every reason to think the job would be his, but his application was turned down because of the label of infidel which was attached to him. It was a crude epithet to which he always vigorously objected.

This failure was not just his loss. He would have made a good teacher as he was controlled in manner and precise in expression, and he did then, and would always, romantically correlate enlightenment of mind with the purifying of one's heart. He later wrote a small book on grammar, also one on his great love, mathematics, which title has a modern ring, *Mathematics No Mystery*; and three others for very young children.

It was the uncertainty of freelance teaching, then all he could hope for, which prompted him in the February of 1838 to followed Frederick Hollick's advice and apply to Robert Owen's Association of All Classes of All Nations for a permanent position. And so Holyoake became an Owenite social missionary, a euphemism for lecturer and propagandist. In this new role, he spent the autumn months of 1840 and most of the following winter and spring at Worcester, sent there through election held at the Association's Congress of 1840.

One of Worcester's more famous visitors, William Cobbett, had said of it in the spring of 1830:

> I have observed in this country, and especially near Worcester, that the working people seem to be better off than in many other parts, one cause of which is, I dare say, that *glove manufacturing* which cannot be carried on by fire or by wind or by water, and which is, therefore, carried on by the *hands* of human beings. It gives work to women and children as well

> as to men; and that work is done... in their cottages, and amidst the fields and hop-gardens... there is no horrible misery here, as at Manchester, Leeds, Glasgow, Paisley, and other Hell-Holes of 84 degrees of heat. [9]

This would have struck a chord with Holyoake. He was not exactly against the factory system; it was progress and he had no quarrel with that except in its selfish application by powerful men. The ways of the independent worker still survived in Worcester as it once had in the loom weavers' cottages of towns like Halifax and Huddersfield, places he had visited. There, a world away from Worcester, working-class independence had vanished into the wheels and cogs, steam and pistons of capitalism.

If Worcester's people suffered less than some, maybe this was why Holyoake found its inhabitants disappointingly uninterested in his social message which, by 1841, was one which openly threw doubt on Christianity as a solution. A small group of Worcester socialists met on Sundays in a lecture room, known in Owenite circles as a Hall of Science, 'not that we had much science', Holyoake commented 'merely a preference for it'. Worcester's Hall of Science was a converted workshop on Garden Street, set up by a local carpenter who, at one meeting, tried some laughing gas, the effect of which sent him turning somersaults 'all down the hall, and downstairs out into the open'. [10]

'Few people in those days knew or believed that stones had a story to tell', Holyoake much later recalled.[11] The very word 'science' was likely to produce deep suspicion in most minds and combined with 'socialist' there was little chance of Holyoake's stay in Worcester going unnoticed. He gave a series of lectures on "The Philosophy of the Human Mind", using illustrations and 'a great variety of skulls, of the human and brute creation', while his other lectures on "Morality and Socialism" demonstrated, according to a well-wisher, a 'high moral and truly religious tone of sentiment', which seemed to be his most 'ardent desire and endeavour to inculcate among his audience'.[12] Opposition to these activities ran so strongly in the majority in Worcester that the private teaching Holyoake did to supplemented his meagre salary he did under the pseudonym of Mr. Jacob to avoid attention.

There is no doubt that those scandalized by the socialist movement would have been greatly alarmed had they heard the first lecture Holyoake gave in Worcester in 1840, when he, twenty-three years old, addressed his audience in these terms:

> Those whose duty it is to cry to heaven against the sufferings of the poor, sing Te Deums in honour of bloody victories, or thank God our Taxes are increased and tell us to be content! They live in luxury, while their professed Master had not, nor the children of their common Father have not, where to lay their heads. *Is this Christianity*? If the poor man asks for his Political rights, he is told he is too ignorant to have them. He is not too ignorant *to toil and starve*, but only to *obtain redress*. But, whatever may be the obstacle, true, useful, practical knowledge is the only infallible means of removing it. The praying of Eighteen Centuries has only left us without even the sign of a better state. Faith without *works* has been very '*dead*'; and we must work out our own salvation. [13]

He probably said much the same to Worcester's Chartists when he addressed them in the New Year. His wife, Ellen, was there to hear him. Holyoake also let out the Hall of Science to this group for a New Year's Eve Ball. None of the city churches was willing to do the same. This event, coming soon after the Birmingham riots and amidst the ensuing physical-force Chartist activity, did not pass without censure from *The Worcester Herald*. Its editor called the evening's entertainments 'immorality and vice'. Holyoake was furious and wrote in the Owenite paper *The New Moral World*:

> we have since been charged as abetters of a "bloody rebellion" for letting the Chartists our room; and in a most "orthodox" way, the tendency (horrid, of course) of our festivals has been laid before the public... The ball was called an "orgie" and though it was held at holiday time and concluded at half-past one, it was deemed truly awful that poor people should be out so late. *They* ought go to bed as soon as they come from work. [14]

His fury was increased by an article on a New Year's Ball held by the local hunt which ran in the same issue of the *Herald* and which approvingly describes how a midnight dinner and festivities had ended no earlier than six in the morning.

Ellen and their baby Madeline had only just joined him in Worcester, having spent the summer and autumn months of 1840 in Birmingham. Before their arrival Holyoake had regularly made the journey to Birmingham to see them and so it was that he knew the long road between the two places very well, having travelled it many times. According to all accounts its aspects were beautiful:

> The state of its cultivation appears to very great advantage, as here are no tracts of any considerable extent, so barren, or so totally neglected, as to be without an agreeable, and profitable verdure. [15]

Now, twelve months on, and once again walking the final stretches of road to Worcester, he would catch glimpses of the great humped, granite spines of the Malvern Hills, still ten or so miles off, rising out of the vale beyond the city and in the exact direction he was headed. He had reached the heart of the Severn plain, the rich soiled meadows and pasture fringing the banks of the river. These meadows are perfect grazing. It is a curious thing that in this year of 1842 imported livestock from Europe into England was first admitted and the people who would be most affected by this event were then so distracted by the fight over the Corn Laws and the rising discontent of the industrial workers, that objections were never raised.

The closer Holyoake came to Worcester the more fields he would see divided by bean and hop poles, all pitched with great regularity and exactness. It was women's work to twist the vines to the poles and secure them with dried rushes in readiness for growth and harvesting in late summer. The weather was good, the scene peaceful, but Holyoake was walking into a storm far deadlier than the one John Angell James and his wife had met on the same road years before. Holyoake knew quite well that his present editorship of a radical newspaper as extreme as the *Oracle of Reason* carried with it the chance of prosecution. The paper's printer, William Chilton, had spelt it out to him in a letter written from Bristol shortly after Southwell's arrest. In it Chilton says, 'There must, I imagine, be a name attached to the *Oracle*', and adds that, though he is no coward, he would prefer it if Holyoake shouldered the inherent risks of editorship. [16]

The approach roads to the City of Worcester passed through considerable gardens and nurseries, also fields of vetch now long gone. To a traveller coming from the north and reaching high ground, the Malvern Hills, seeming hardly any nearer viewed from Perdiswell at Worcester's northern outskirts than they do ten miles farther off, rise up again, beautifully and rather strangely, from the horizon. And many of the buildings Holyoake passed as he entered the city that day still stand, seagulls wheeling and crying above their roofs as they did in 1842, and in much greater numbers then because Worcester, built alongside the eastern bank of the Severn, was a thriving inland port.

Holyoake arrived on Sunday, the 22nd of May, as the city was getting over its celebration of the approval of the Severn Navigation Bill. Two days earlier

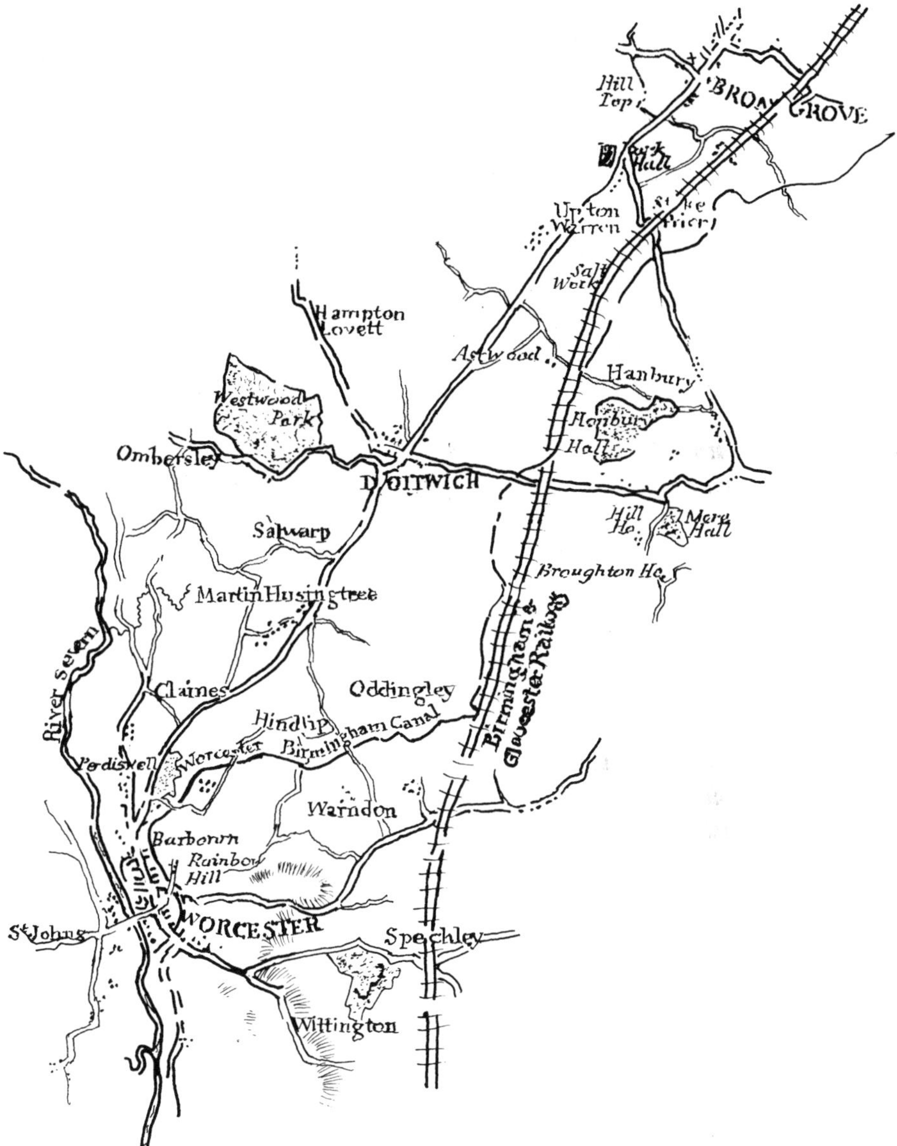
BROMSGROVE
Hill Top
Upton Warren
Stoke Prior
Salt Works
Hampton Lovett
Astwood
Hanbury
Westwood Park
Hanbury Hall
Ombersley
DROITWICH
Hill Ho.
Mere Hall
Salwarp
Broughton Ho.
Martin Husingtree
Birmingham & Gloucester Railway
River Severn
Claines
Oddingley
Hindlip
Birmingham Canal
Perdiswell
Worcester
Warndon
Barbourn
Rainbow Hill
St Johns
WORCESTER
Spetchley
Wittington

the scheme's promoters and supporters had had the city's church bells ring for the whole of that day, a clamour Holyoake's ears missed by only a few hours. The Severn runs wide at Worcester, but do not imagine today's serene giant of a river, then it was one of the country's great commercial highways, and Worcester owed its existence to its traffic. The railway had yet to come to the city, and for as long as it stayed away the Severn remained its commercial lifeline from the Bristol Channel to the Black Country and beyond. 'Its channel' says a contemporary observer, 'is generally eighty, or one hundred yards wide, sometimes much more, and four, five, or six yards deep… and has been navigated with barges of about sixty tons burden, for time immemorial', and upon it came and went coal and steel, press gangs and disease.[17]

The Severn had almost claimed the life of Robert Owen when, as a boy, he had come close to taking a fatal fall into its waters from the back of his father's pony while crossing the bridge at Newtown. Its waters flow strong and deep at Newtown although many miles upstream. The fall knocked him unconscious and, miraculously it seemed to him, when he came to he found himself alive and dry upon the bridge. Now George Jacob Holyoake had met this great river's flow. Within twenty-four hours he would leave it to walk on to Cheltenham where the climax of his journey's course, now closely knit with national trends of dispute and revolt, would begin.

7

In all probability Holyoake stayed at Worcester for one night only, even though the lecture planned for Cheltenham was not for another two days. A walk he had made not long before, from Sheffield to Huddersfield, had taught him that too much physical exercise is not conducive to the delivery of a good speech soon afterwards. To avoid a repetition of this, enough time for rest before the lecture at Cheltenham would be his likely plan. This was not his first visit to Cheltenham. He, Ellen and their baby Madeline, had spent a short and decidedly miserable time there in the bitterly cold January of the previous year, during his Owenite posting to Worcester. Lodging with hosts who provided neither food nor water, Holyoake had lost his way through dark, slippery streets in search of something for them to eat and drink. His impression of Cheltenham was of a place:

> ... where everything is genteel and thin. The people... are like the supernumeraries on a stage... their clothes are decent, but they cannot properly be said to wear them; they carry them about on their backs to show that they have such things. In the same manner eating and drinking is rather pantomime than reality. [1]

Holyoake was not the only one to feel this way about mid-nineteenth century Cheltenham. The town did not always enjoy a good press. Among detractors was William Cobbett who, in 1821, said of it:

> Cheltenham is a nasty, ill-looking place, half clown and half cockney. The town is one street, there are rows of white tenements, with green balconies, like those inhabited by the tax-eaters round London. Indeed, this place appears to be the residence of an assemblage of tax-eaters... Soon after quitting this resort of the lame and the lazy, the gormandising and guzzling, the bilious and the nervous, we proceeded on... [2]

By 'tax-eaters' Cobbett meant those who 'drew their wealth from the interest on enormous loans to the government which had to be repaid out of taxes upon the poor'.[3]

So, after a night spent at Worcester, Holyoake was not looking forward with cheerful anticipation to his arrival at Cheltenham as he walked the twenty-five miles of country between it and Worcester the next morning. At least it was a warm spring day, and the Malvern Hills, brightened by the morning sun, would be a pleasant travelling companion for some time yet for, keeping more or less ten miles east of them, he would walk their length and more before reaching Tewkesbury. Not only the Malverns to his right but to his left rose Bredon Hill which, said Cobbett, 'looks over the counties of Worcester, Gloucester, Hereford and part of Warwick, and the rich part of Stafford' and from which you can see 'one of the very richest spots of England'.[4] Within this richest of spots lying within the Severn Vale are the villages of Kempsey, some seven miles south of Worcester, Severn Stoke and Ryall, lying close to the Severn's eastern banks. Holyoake's road took him through each of these and was bounded by hedges 'full of timber and particularly very fine elm' also of 'hawthorn, smooth woods, bramble and the Burnet rose plant...' and which intersected 'orchards with all kinds of fruit trees'. One observer of the time says of the country through which Holyoake passed that day:

> There is in the air and climate of these parts of Worcestershire, a mildness, softness, and salubrity, which brings to perfection the fruits of the earth a full fortnight earlier than in the country thirty miles north, insomuch, that it has been usual for reapers, from Cheshire and Lancashire, to assist in the reaping of Worcestershire... and to get home in time for that of their own country. [5]

Cobbett had stayed in Ryall thirty years earlier as the guest of Mr. John Price, an avid and successful breeder of Hereford cattle and whose reputation in this field remained unrivalled in the country. As Holyoake walked through Ryall, from where Mr Price had recently retreated across the river to live in Poole House at Upton-upon-Severn, he might have given some thought to the cattle and sheep thereabouts and, were he aware of the fact, would have noted the herds' recovery from a recent and prolonged case of foot and mouth disease.

From Ryall the road to Tewkesbury crosses over into Gloucestershire then continues on through Naunton before arriving at the banks of the River Avon. Once over the Avon, Tewkesbury is reached. From there, if he took the most southerly route, Holyoake would pass Guston Field, Combe Hill, Knightsford,

Ukington and the fields thereabouts which Cobbett describes as 'ploughed in ridges about 20 feet wide' the angle of which 'is pretty nearly as sharp as that of some slated roofs of houses', before sensing the presence of Cheltenham up ahead. It was a long journey, he would be tired and perhaps, at this point, experiencing a momentary foreboding, if not prescient then produced by recollection of his far from happy visit sixteen months earlier.

Cheltenham had enjoyed huge popularity as a spa town since the turn of the century and as a consequence its population had swelled from three thousand to thirty-eight thousand during the intervening years. In 1841 it could boast four major spa buildings, the original and the Pitville with its multi-coloured portico facing the roadway, the Montpellier and Cambray. It was a place of boulevards, of distinct and elegant architecture. The community supported twelve physicians and no fewer than thirty practising surgeons. Its rise, then, had been meteoric and civic pride had grown proportionately. However, the town's reputation was threatened for there was a wicked rumour abroad in London that the waters were not genuine.[6]

Holyoake knew he was approaching a community particularly hostile to resident and visiting socialists. Cheltenham's clerics, traders, businessmen and similarly placed others, of whom there were many, took the infant term 'socialism' to mean anything that smacked of religious infidelity, of everything pernicious and anarchic. The vanguard of those holding this view was led by the minister of the town's parish church, Francis Close.

Over the many years of his ministry at Cheltenham, Francis Close transformed the town into an Evangelical stronghold. No surprise then to find him leading local opposition to rail travel on Sunday, theatrical entertainments at all times, also the singing of oratorios (as using the Word of God as entertainment), and to the races. His fears for his community's moral well-being did not extend to the growing popularity of spiritualism or Table-Turning, an art, dark some believed, which he dismissed as deriving from neither evil nor good inspiration. He was an implacable enemy of Popery and, of course, Socialism. Like John Angell James, Francis Close had a strong presence and magnificent voice. Many were drawn to him. Some would discreetly compete over the gaining of his regard through the giving of gifts and favours. Despite his community's solicitous care of him Close was inclined to periods of exhaustion, remedied by complete rest in the countryside.

'There he is, then', observed one who knew him, 'with a quick and somewhat rolling gait, half-sailor like..., trudging down Bay's Hill, carrying his Bible in a leather case with a loop handle, his little wife on his arm, to St. Mary's... looking very eager and very happy, as though going to a work he loved.'[7] His admirers

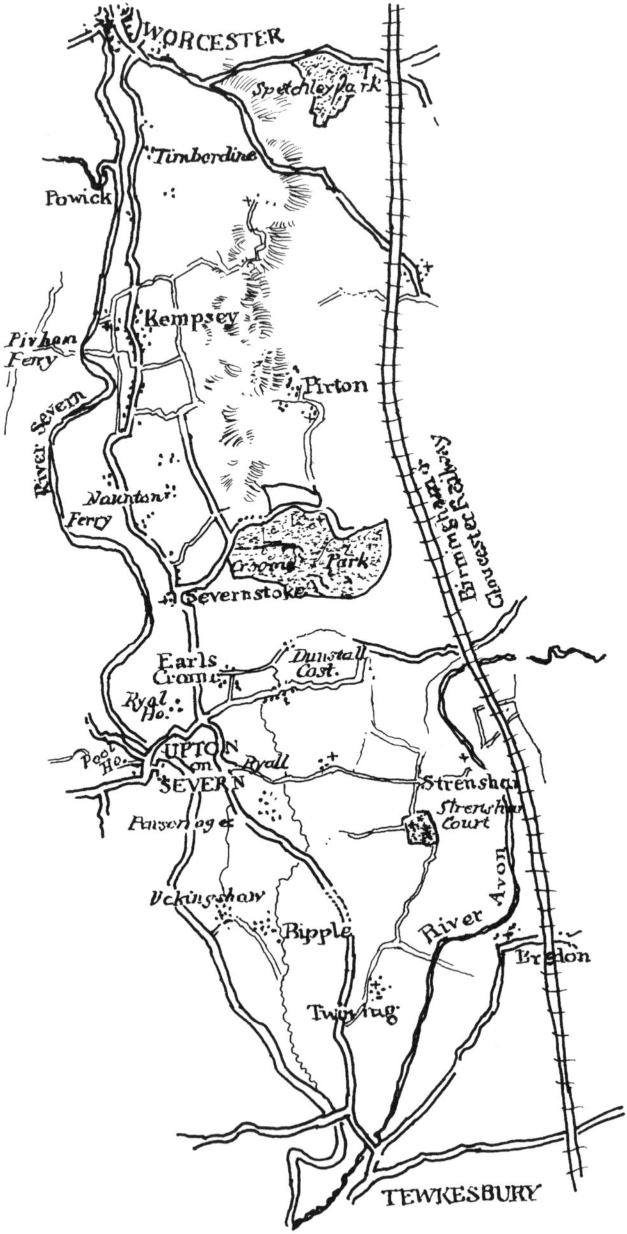
WORCESTER
Spetchley Park
Timberdine
Powick
Kempsey
Ferry
River Severn
Pirton
Birmingham & Gloucester Railway
Naunton
Ferry
Croome Park
Severnstoke
Earls Croome
Dunstall Cast.
Ryal Ho.
Pool Ho.
UPTON on SEVERN
Ryall
Strensham
Strensham Court
Parsonage
Uckingshaw
Ripple
River Avon
TEWKESBURY

and those less admiring agreed on one thing: he was Cheltenham's 'ruling spirit', its 'presiding genius', its 'dominant power'.[8] Close's ministry hung upon 'the sufficiency of Holy Scripture to make each man wise unto salvation…'. This he elucidated in his first sermon as perpetual curate to St. Mary's flock in 1826:

> Observe, I. WHAT THE MINSTERS OF GOD DO NOT PREACH – "they do not preach themselves"; II. CONSIDER WHAT THEY DO PREACH – "Christ Jesus the Lord"; and III. SEE THE CHARACTER IN WHICH THEY DESIRE TO LIVE AND DIE AMONG YOU – "ourselves your servants for Jesus' sake". [9]

Even so, Close's influence on the town of Cheltenham was not of so nugatory a composition, nor so selflessly applied as this pledge suggests. That is not to say he did not truly believe in carrying out his ministerial role as a passive channel of God's Word. So strong was the reliance on the infallibility of the Bible that no church minister need assume his position as it was invested in him through the authority of God's revelation. Well might he and others so blessed be happy as they set about their work, for the path ahead was clear: to bring into force the beneficent authority of the church upon the people, and so bring each to God's love and secure souls for the world to come. Attention to the inequities of the present world was not the issue and would remain so for decades to come.

This is why Francis Close could stand before his congregation that day in 1826 to apologise, in advance of the fact, for an obligation upon him 'to withdraw, in great measure, from that intercourse with my parishioners which might otherwise be desirable… I mean the proper visitation of the sick and dying, in a parish so widely scattered. I shall prove that it is not indifference, nor spiritual pride, nor any unworthy motive that drives me into a more retired life, but the great and almost overwhelming responsibilities which devolve upon me'.[10] Church and its business was the overwhelming responsibility. Pastoral care was not the pressing responsibility of the day, things would have to get much worse for the labouring classes before that would happen.

St Mary's is a beautiful church standing where Christians have worshipped for twelve hundred years. One Sunday morning soon after the Birmingham Bull Ring riots of 1839 St Mary's was overwhelmed by a large assembly of male Chartists who filled the pews accustomed to accommodating the respectable tradesman, solicitor, surgeon, hotelier, his wife and family of Cheltenham. For one morning the church was made to play hostess to a militant group of reformers and radicals, predominantly from the industrious classes, who thought it a good advertisement of their cause to take her over. Close, forewarned of the plan, cancelled a prior engagement so that he might preach to this congregation.

In his 'fine rich voice' and employing his 'great force of will, remarkable and restless energy, deep religious earnestness',[11] he chastised the men sitting before him: '*"Consider how great things the Lord hath done for you!"*... Has it been all wrath, all unkindness, all judgment with you? impossible! You must be blind to the hand of God!':

> God has fed you, and you have forgotten to lift your heart in gratitude when he showered his blessings on you. You have clothed yourself with his garments, you have spent his money, and enjoyed his time, but you have forgotten Him from whom all goodness flows! [12]

'And is it possible' he went on, 'that any one can be so ignorant or so wilfully blind as to deny that there has been a special providence over Great Britain, and that special mercies have been poured down on her?... Therefore, I say, have nothing to do with that vile system of Socialism... [it] is rebellion against God because it takes the Bible out of the hands of men, and puts a mock bible in its place... under the pretence of having discovered a new moral world'.[13]

It can be taken by this speech that Francis Close did not perceive the realities of the lives of the working men before him, a failing which would not have recommended his message to them. And his confusion of Socialism with Chartism would add distance between preacher and congregation, the two movements being distinct and sometimes mutually wary entities. Where Chartism presented problems for the Socialists in its tendency to alienate influential establishment figures from the aims both parties pursued, Owen's Socialism appeared to the Chartists to be irrational in its insistence upon communal property and colony life.

The following Sunday, August 25th, 1839, a group of women Chartists followed the men's example and were treated to a second sermon in which they were reminded that woman is the source of all human sin and must expect to suffer. Close concluded with the opinion that armed insurrection by the working classes, of the sort seen during the Bull Ring riots the month before, could never be justified, aimed as it was 'against their country, their Queen and their God!... property, life, liberty, and everything we possess is endangered [by it]'.[14]

Not until the organ struck up and the National Anthem played, did the visiting Chartists stand to leave.

8

As Francis Close went about his business, another prelate of greater determination and prominence was, at this time, preparing evidence against the Owenite socialists. His name was Henry Phillpotts, Bishop of Exeter, who, as a member of the House of Lords, would seek an enquiry into the activities of the Society of Religious Rationalists. Henry Phillpotts was a man considerably more dangerous to the socialist cause than half-a-dozen Francis Closes or John Brindleys. With a predator's skill he pursued many unfortunates throughout his career, wielding his powers as bishop with great flair and aplomb. If John Angell James is representative of theologians who could not hold the hearts of religious aspirants like George Jacob Holyoake, Henry Phillpotts, Bishop of Exeter, exemplifies a side to the Christian clergy as it then existed which drew the rage and sealed the disaffection of such men.

Born into a Somerset family, Henry Phillpotts was educated at Gloucester's Cathedral School and matriculated at Oxford in 1791 at the age of thirteen. Possessing, then, great mental ability and later a well connected wife, he early in his career attracted the good fortune to be presented with two Crown livings, Kilmserdon near Bath and Stainton-le-Street, Durham, though he lived at neither. By the time he was thirty-one his 'rapid advancement continued with the collation to the ninth prebendal stall in Durham Cathedral', where, with 'considerable skill and tact' he controlled hostile elements within his vestry and gave evidence 'of a capacity to be displayed in later years'.[1]

His physical attributes, according to one not an admirer, included a 'rather bulging forehead, restless twinkling blue eyes, a proud curving nose, and a rat-trap mouth whose corners drooped in line with a crescent of deep wrinkles extending from his nostrils to his chin'. Portraiture bears out the description. He was 'a small man, but his every movement betrayed energy and impatience'.[2] At the passing of the Reform Act of 1832 which he opposed, and over which his effigy was burned at Durham, he delivered to the House of Lords a speech 'full of fire and venom, very able'. Then he was described simply as a man with 'a desperate and dreadful countenance, and looks like the man he is'.[3]

The year 1819 finds Phillpotts sitting on a committee to consider Owen's social proposals and also joining the debate on new Poor Law regulations. Owen would not have disagreed with Phillpotts' view that 'the great desideratum of all is to find some method of reanimating the spirit of proper independence in the lower orders' but would have parted company with him on his method which was to induce the working classes 'to struggle hard'. Phillpotts reckoned that to make life easier for the working man was as good as to invite him to depend upon the parish, to 'familiarize himself... with the prospect of being a pauper, to connect it with all his plans of industry or idleness – in short, to associate the notion of [human] right'.[4]

Phillpotts was not entirely ignorant of the realities of pauperism or the labourer's plight. In 1812, while at Durham, he received a letter in which an employee of the Wallsend colliery took great pains to describe a pit-child's life. 'I feel great diffidence' the writer begins, 'in venturing an opinion', and then goes on to explain how:

> At the age of six or seven years, with a few exceptions, the boys are taken into the pit, where they are employed underground from ten to fourteen, and frequently sixteen hours a day... the hours of cessation from labour are barely sufficient for taking sleep and refreshment, and for a considerable part of the year, those employed in *single shift* pits never see daylight except three days in fourteen... It is, however, worthy of remark, that after having passed the above period in total ignorance in point of education, that many, by dint of application, learn to read and write. [5]

Among the ranks of those with the power to change things, Henry Phillpotts was far from alone in viewing these social abominations as acceptable; the prevailing economic philosophy of the time was an apology for the fact. In this regard he believed the likes of Robert Owen's movement to have brought the country to an 'age of excessive sensibility' where the poor, illiterate and hard-worked might be seen as victims, their employers as exploiters.

Nor was he alone in his practice of holding valuable benefices without ever actively attending them, and becoming very rich as a result. He was, perhaps, singular in his outspokenness and in his attempts to repress the outspokenness of others. Once safely installed in the Bishop's Palace at Exeter in 1831, he commenced to pursue the ruin of a local journalist called Thomas Latimer, dubbed Cobbett of the West. Latimer had been a student in London with the Chartist William Lovett and it is no surprise to find controversy and eventual litigation occur between Phillpotts and the young man. Following Phillpottic machinations concerning the desperate fate of an unfortunate curate, Latimer accused the bishop in *The Western Times* of being 'a brawler', and called him 'a consecrated, careless perverter of the fact, and one who does no credit to the mitre, which he is paid £200 a week or thereabouts, to wear'.[6]

Evidence bears out the spirit of Latimer's accusations, for despite his bishop's mitre Phillpotts was not above acts of nepotism and, thwarted in his purpose to appoint his son, John, to a Precentorship in the cathedral at £1,200 a year (and 'with nice pickings' according to Latimer), he promptly appointed a friend to the Precentorship of Worcester which was at once vacated by this man, leaving the living free for John. But the one event which most damaged his reputation with the people of Exeter involved his conduct during the cholera epidemic of 1832. For the duration of the crisis the Bishop commenced a confirmation tour of his vast diocese, returning to its epicentre, Exeter, only once and very briefly in August. One of his archdeacons wrote that 'the Bishop came unexpectedly from Teignmouth, sat in his throne, but spoke to no one, had no sermon, and did nothing – which has made the people more indignant at his conduct than before'. In Exeter, four hundred people died of cholera between July and October that year. The Bishop's view at the time was that 'watching the interests of the Church in Parliament and in the public mind generally, form the most difficult and most distressing part of a Bishop's duty'.[7]

Henry Phillpotts seems to have been curiously insensitive to himself and to others, and the attention of this strangely nerveless, clever and indomitable man did eventually turn upon the socialist and reform movements of the time, and especially upon Robert Owen and his Society of Rational Religionists. In the February of 1840 an eight page pamphlet appeared for distribution: 'Important Correspondence between the Bishop of Exeter! Lord Melbourne! and the noted Robert Owen! Concerning his late visit to the Queen, and Abominable designs to tamper with her marriage with Prince Albert'.[8]

Lord Melbourne, prime minister at the time, had introduced Robert Owen to Victoria some months earlier. Owen had wanted to bring to the Queen's attention his views on marriage, which were that marriage is an unnatural state and that there should be recourse to divorce for the poor as for the rich on the grounds that to be trapped in an unhappy marriage is the cause of deception, promiscuity and crime. The conventional family group was inward looking and too prone to selfishness, while communitarianism, by which man, wife and child could share their lives with others rather than live in competition was, Owen believed, self-evidently a better form for the moral development of society.

On the 24th of January, 1840, the Bishop made his way to the Painted Chamber at Westminster (where their lordships sat during the building of Barry's new Houses of Parliament) carrying with him a petition signed by four thousand of Birmingham's clergy, bankers, merchants and manufacturers. His petition was the result of considerable planning, its purpose to bring to public attention 'the horrible effects of Robert Owen's baneful system'. Phillpotts began by telling the assemble lords how these petitioners, "lament the great impetus which has been given to Socialism by the presentation to Her Majesty at her court of Robert Owen last year". But he was interrupted by Henry Brougham, life-long friend of Owen, who came late into the chamber. The Bishop rejoiced, he said, "at the interruption... whether regular or not".[9] Brougham had with him four petitions of his own, three from socialist bodies and one from Owen. That Owen would welcome a public enquiry was something Phillpotts had not worked into his calculations.

At the start of his career, in 1810, Henry Brougham had successfully defended Leigh Hunt against the Attorney-General's charge of seditious libel for publishing an article condemning military flogging, and he ever remained his own man: a 'spare man with a long upturned nose and a compressed mouth'. His habitual impatience with the proceedings of the House manifested itself 'in the constant crossing and recrossing of his legs and by his most notorious mannerism, the twitching of his nose'.[10] He now tells the House that Robert Owen welcomes the setting up of a committee to inquire into his socialist principles.

Phillpotts' reply was to suggest that Lord Brougham "should move for a committee". Brougham had no intention of moving for an inquiry because, he explained, he was not partisan, he was not a socialist. "The noble and learned lord is too wise and good to be one", said the Bishop who then went on to explain to the House his objections to the socialists in these terms: "If bodies of men", he says, "combine together in different parts of the kingdom, and call into operation societies in various quarters for the special purpose of altering the common law of the land, and of effecting an irreligious and immoral object, can such proceedings be considered in any other light than as a grievous infraction of the law?"[11]

Brougham, having every confidence in the good sense of his countrymen, thought the socialists could safely be 'left to themselves', unless the country were to see 'any attempt made to put them down by force'. If that were to happen, "do not", he said "over-rate the powers of persecution to inculcate doctrines which nothing but persecution could spread".[12]

Present at this sitting was the Marquis of Normanby who agreed with Brougham: "Whatever might be the intentions of the right reverend prelate, I do not think that the effects of his proceedings would be any other than to promulgate more widely these doctrines of socialism". Phillpotts' intentions included causing Lord Melbourne embarrassment. It was widely known he had a huge disliking for the prime minister who now stood to 'disclaim the inference' that he was sympathetic to Robert Owen's views just because he had presented him to the young Victoria, it had been performed as a 'formal office' he said.

It was left to a Tory and supporter of the Bishop, the elderly Duke of Wellington, to thank Phillpotts for the 'proofs he had produced of the dangerous tendency of the doctrines' inculcated by the socialists.

The next week found the Bishop speaking again in the House of Lords, this time on the dangers of an unchecked, radical press (to which number *The Oracle of Reason* would soon be added by the unwary Charles Southwell). Stamp duty on newspapers was not enough to keep socialist papers in check according to Phillpotts. Additional clauses to the present law would enable government more effectively to suppress unstamped publications aimed at the working classes: "The law of the land", he said, "has wisely armed Government with the means of putting down such publications without bringing them before the attention of the people... The Government never can be justified in permitting... the diffusion of any opinion blasphemously injurious to that God by whom princes reign and decree justice. The Socialists believe in no religion, which is the sole foundation on which the Government stands. The whole frame of society rests upon religion".

He spoke again of the Owenites, giving information gathered over many months, aided in part by John Brindley. He describes to the House the organization and affairs of the Society of Rational Religionists, telling of the suicide of a youth, depressed, he says, by the pernicious effects of the socialist influence. He quotes a colourful Owenite speech full of blasphemy, blood and barbarism, given in Birmingham by Charles Southwell, and reads John Brindley's report of a visit made to Owen's Queenswood Community where he had witnessed a parody of church service. Holyoake himself describes how social missionaries were sometimes asked to 'name' children in a kind of mimicry of Christian baptism.

All that resulted from the Bishop of Exeter's campaign against the country's rising social movement was an instruction by the House to the Lords' Lieutenant to direct all town magistrates to be alert to publications of a blasphemous nature and to prosecute everything of a seditious nature. This was a bad turn of events for the Owenites. Many felt that their leader had let a golden opportunity for publicity slip away in not more aggressively challenging the Bishop. There would be no public discussion, while their activities would, from this time, be scrutinized more closely by the authorities.

Charles Southwell, making his own challenge, addressed a pamphlet to the Bishop in which he called Phillpotts 'mad' and accused him of reasoning 'from principles that have no reality out of [his] own diseased imagination'.[13] Owen was too well positioned within the ranks of the ruling elite for Phillpotts' attack to threaten him directly, but it left men like George Jacob Holyoake and Charles Southwell vulnerable to censure and prosecution. In the small towns it encouraged figures like the Reverend Francis Close who, already alert to the situation, would be very interested in the arrival in his town of the young social missionary George Jacob Holyoake.

9

And so it was into an antagonistic atmosphere that George Jacob Holyoake, arrived in Cheltenham to deliver his lecture at the Mechanics' Institution on 'Home Colonization' on Tuesday evening, 24th of May. Cheltenham was not the town and Holyoake, after the recent treatment of Charles Southwell in Bristol, not in a sufficiently composed state of mind for following events to pass smoothly. It was known by some in Cheltenham that this young man was the present editor of the *Oracle of Reason*. It is not at all surprising to find the town's magistrates waiting for him.

He knew a number of people in Cheltenham by this time, and probably stayed with George and Harriet Adams and their children in their terraced house on King Street, from which it was a ten minutes' walk to the Mechanics' Institution building on Albion Street.

Picture a young man, clean-shaven with a head of brown hair falling in one sweep to his collar, slight of build, speaking in a rather poor, reedy voice to an audience of some one hundred men and women on 'Home Colonization' and you have an image of George Jacob Holyoake on that May evening. A board had been erected over the door of the Mechanics' Institution advertising the evening's attraction, and the presence of antagonists would not have surprised the speaker. Some not so sympathetic to his message had attended his Sheffield lectures earlier in the year and he fully expected the same now. On this night, a young printer named James Bartram, employed by the *Cheltenham Chronicle*, came to the meeting with a friend from work. They arrived late at the crowded hall, at about nine o'clock, when Holyoake was in full flow on Owenite policies on communitarian colonization. The drift of his speech went something like this:

"Poor rates and pauperism is increasing – it is now no dishonour to ask for relief – the working man suffers through the lowering in value of human labour – the present government has the power but not the will – knowledge is power – ignorance and poverty being the chief causes of crime, education is essential to the prosperity of the country and to the independence of the working man – moral power elevates where wealth degrades – wealth is a new god and lords it over all others – socialism has solutions which can bring great advantage to society as a whole – we propose to set up self-supporting colonies, to purchase land, erect buildings, stock farms paid for by capital without interest* – the colonist's reward for hard work is his pride – Home Colonies will provide the means to a just and wise system of production and distribution".[1]

When finished he invited questions. The voice of one Mr. Maitland came up from the floor. "You have spoken a great deal about our duty to man, but what of our duty to God – are there to be no chapels in your community?" [2]

It is difficult to say how prepared Holyoake was for a question of this kind, but he knew the danger in it. He could answer in one of two ways: express his feelings honestly and lay himself open to the charge of disbelief, or evade and be considered a moral coward. Neither option was attractive, especially the latter. Having but a moment to consider his answer, and being not 'much skilled in policy', and feeling that 'when a man cannot take care of consequences, he ought to take care of the credit of his cause', he spoke his mind. In recent months he had been advocating the separation of theology from socialist principles in public discussion, and so the following, which supports this underlying principle, is probably an accurate recollection of his reply to Mr. Maitland. This is what he says he remembers of it:

"As you, sir, have introduced religion into this meeting, which I have carefully avoided in my lecture, I will answer frankly... Home colonization is an economical scheme, and as we can ill bear the burden of a god here, he may lie rather heavy upon their hands there. Our national debt and our national taxation hang like millstones round the neck of the poor man's prosperity, saying nothing of the enormous gatherings of capitalists... and in the face of our misery and want, we are charged twenty millions more for the worship of God. This is utilitarianism versus divinity; and I appeal to your heads and your pockets if we are not too poor to have a god? If poor men cost the state half so much, they would be put like officers upon half-pay. I think while our distress lasts it would be wise to do the same thing with the deity".

Maybe some in the audience gave a laugh at this. If they did, it did not help Holyoake when his time came to answer for it. Almost certainly the young speaker

* Owen included rewards for the investing capitalist, but Holyoake was not in favour of capitalist money at this time, although he converted to the idea in the 1850s.

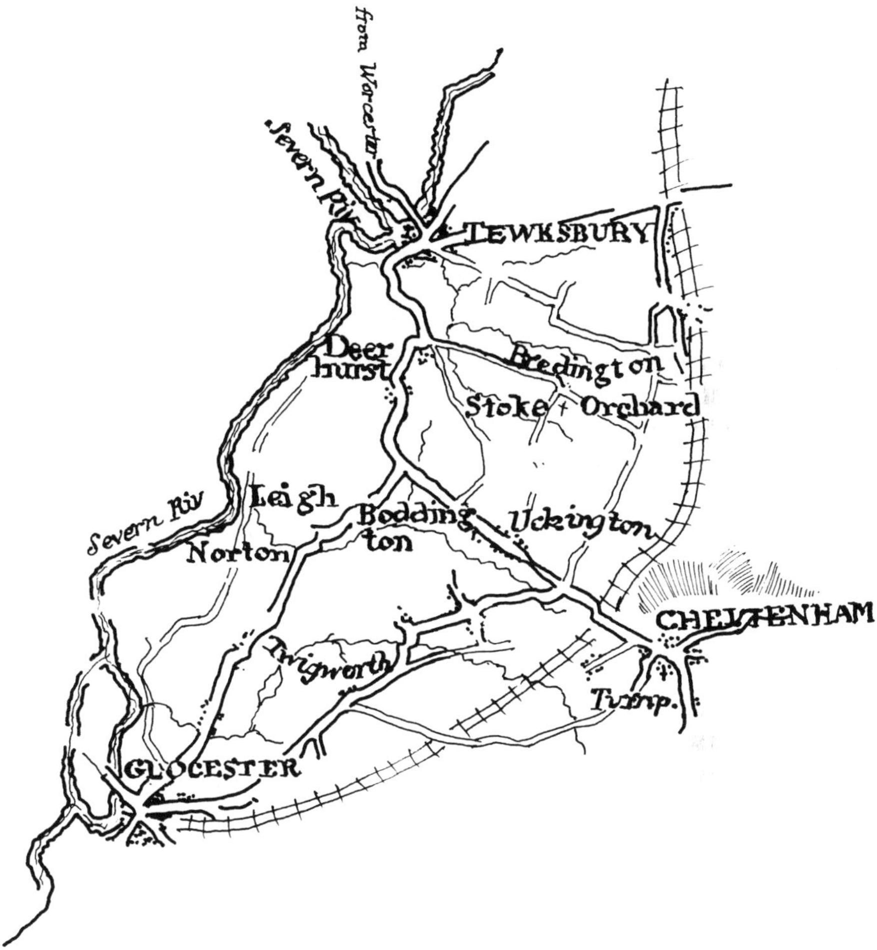
from Worcester
Severn Riv
TEWKSBURY
Deer hurst
Bredington
Stoke Orchard
Leigh
Severn Riv
Norton
Bodding ton
Uckington
CHELTENHAM
Twigworth
Turnp.
GLOCESTER

did not intend to amuse. A letter he had written to the Reverend Wake of Worcester some months earlier bears this out: 'Do not think', he told Mr. Wake,

> That because I seem to speak lightly that I therefore think jestingly on the great question of religion. I do not... I was once religious in your sense of the term, and do know something about it. [3]

Holyoake's proposal to separate religion from the socialist message had received a rebuff from his colleague, Henry Jeffrey. 'Socialism teaches certain views of human nature', Jeffrey had written to him in March from Edinburgh:

> And there again it must come into collision with popular faiths. If as a society we shrink from encountering the religious world we shall be treated as hypocrites or cowards, we shall fail in meeting the demands of the age, and shall fall to pieces in consequence of such treachery to our own cause. [4]

"I am not religious", continued Holyoake in answer to Mr. Maitland's question, "my creed is to have no creed. All religion has been driven out of me... But what do I hear? That morality cannot exist without religion! Preposterous! Religion, in my opinion has ever poisoned the fountain springs of morality... look at its bloody instruments of torture and its fell subjugation of honesty when man would shun the revolting homage it demands; and there we read its character!... I shudder at the thought of religion, I flee the bible as a viper, and revolt at the touch of a Christian – for their tender mercies may next fall upon my head!" [5]

A good number of the crowd rewarded this speech with applause and sounds of jocularity before turning out into the darkened street and making for home. James Bartram made his way out with everyone else and the following morning went into work at the printing room of the *Cheltenham Chronicle* (a paper which supported the Reverend Close's views), where his colleagues chafed him over his report of the Holyoake speech. Everyone seemed to think it entertaining but the suggestion of ridicule when speaking of God was to make matters worse for Holyoake when the Cheltenham magistrates moved against him, which they quickly did, for speaking against church and religion.

10

From Cheltenham, Holyoake was faced with a walk of more than thirty miles before he would reach Bristol. The way took him across countryside in a south-westerly direction, passing over the Gloucester-Cirencester crossroads then on to Painswick and Stroud. It was hot weather and the air would be alive with flying insects and birds, the ground bursting with green growth and animal life. He might have heard an early cuckoo. Passing through all this abundance, would he have been aware of the deprivation which many of the local people were suffering? He might have read or heard of the decline in the woollen industry in these parts, the brunt of which was shouldered by the hand loom weavers and their families. A report on the industry's demise, commissioned by the government, had advised that workers be left to suffer as best they could the vagaries of market forces, and the suffering was felt in instances of dreadful deprivation. Holyoake would pass along the ridge of Symonds Hall Hill before walking into Wootton-under-Edge, where the working people were hard hit by unemployment, and then would continue on to Iron Acton before reaching Bristol.

Holyoake liked Bristol and said that he 'was never so happy in any town'. He was greatly impressed by Bristol Bridge which he used as a focal point, and if he walked along the banks of the Avon far enough west he would have seen the two great towers which would, eventually, support Brunel's Egyptian-inspired suspension bridge. The Bristol docks were busy with another Brunel construction, the immense iron steam ship *The Great Britain*. Still in her lock, the vessel was a huge hulk of 3,600 tons and 1,000 horsepower, with a hull containing 60,000 rivets. Once released onto the open seas she would look sleek under steam.

He was reunited with Charles Southwell at the gaol on the Cumberland Road and spent three full days there, from Thursday the 26th, to Saturday the 28th of May, where Southwell's living conditions were maintained to a bearable level with financial help from Thomas Whiting, a Bristol man, and some funds from the London-based Anti-Persecution Union, administered by Maltus Ryall. Saying that, the winter months must have been very difficult for

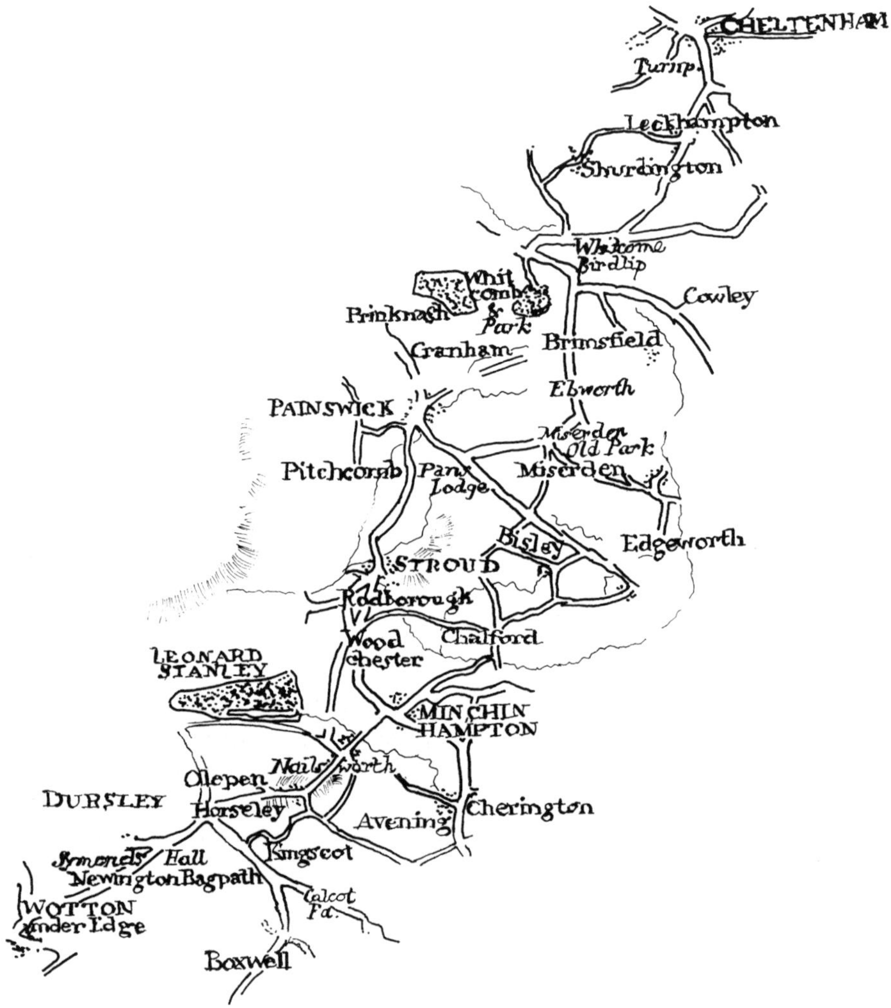
CHELTENHAM
Turnp.
Leckhampton
Shurdington
Whitcome
Birdlip
Whitcombe
&
Park
Cowley
Brinknash
Cranham
Brimsfield
Elworth
PAINSWICK
Miserden
Old Park
Pitchcomb
Miserden
Edgeworth
Bisley
STROUD
Rodborough
Chalford
Wood
chester
LEONARD
STANLEY
MINCHIN
HAMPTON
Nailsworth
Olepen
DURSLEY
Horseley
Avening
Cherington
Kingscot
Symonds Hall
Newington Bagpath
Calcot
Fa.
WOTTON
under Edge
Boxwell

the prisoner as they had been particularly harsh. Southwell was very pleased to see Holyoake. He had written a letter a few months earlier from his cell in his wild, rushed handwriting which seems just to have kept up with his thoughts: 'I will gladly link my fortune with yours or rather my poverty – there is no man I ever met with whom I would sooner live or sooner die'. He wrote this shortly after his arrest and during Holyoake's early support of him. Southwell was in a highly emotional state at the time and, writing in the *Oracle*, says that nothing his accusers could do could make him cry, but the kindness of his friends brought tears to his eyes. Of his trial he had written to Holyoake:

> The judge in my case could have put me down at any moment – if he had adjudged that instead of being permitted to defend myself I should be taken and hanged *in* the court there would have been no opposition – such a blackish pigheaded set of jurymen surely never were seen. [1]

Charles Southwell was a Londoner, a man of emotional and physical energy, quick to feel, unsettled. Creative and equally destructive, thinking through his nerve-ends, his life rebounded from one plot to another as its supports shifted around him. 'I am', he wrote, 'one of those who may be fairly classed among atoms of the fidgets'.[2] Maybe it was Holyoake's steadiness which attracted him. It was a quality he did not possess himself and he may have found comfort in its presence in others.

Southwell's father was seventy-six years old when his son was born, a man three-times-married and progenitor of thirty-three children. Charles was the last of them. His mother, Fanny, had been a servant in the household during the lifetime of the second wife, and her youngest child, from being quite small, had the upper hand of her. Southwell tells us that his father worked as a designer of musical instruments for Broadwood & Sons and was responsible for the 'Cabinet Pianoforte, the upright Grand, the additional keys and those almost forgotten instruments the Harpsichord and Camrichord'.[3] His father was critical of the church and did not conceal his distrust of the local clergy. This paternal sentiment impressed itself upon the young Charles. Whenever the family was visited by a priest the father would tell Fanny to "see to the money draw and lock up the cupboards".[4]

As a boy, Southwell fought other boys in London's Georgian streets and read Hume, Smollett, Gibbon, 'and accounts of the manners, customs, ceremonies, opinions, and prejudices of the various nations constituting this Bedlam of the Universe'.[5] After the death of his aged father, which came before

Southwell's twelfth birthday, he too went to work at Broadwoods as a finisher. The work was nothing more than a flog to him and the years he spent at it were ones of 'misery and utter disgust of life'.[6] It was at Broadwoods that a fellow worker handed him a book of sermons written by Timothy Dwight* and this would prove to be a turning point in Southwell's spiritual progress. Having received negative influences in religious matters at home, he had nonetheless picked up more positive impressions from somewhere:

> The person of Christ... was associated in my childish imagination with the idea of a respectable-looking man, in snuff-coloured coat and rays of glory around his head. I also connected him with a certain street in which I often played... called Stephen-street, where, strange to say, I thought he lived. [7]

But his mind became focused when he read Dwight's sermons on predestination, by which, he took it, God is the single source of our salvation and damnation too:

> I paused and in terrified astonishment literally gasped for breath. "What," I thought after recovering my presence of mind, "is it indeed true that the power, the will, the wish to resist God is supplied and supported by himself. And can it be true that he will eternally punish for a resistance himself has caused?" [8]

And so religion was to be no comfort, nor was his family for although he had innumerable relatives none seems to have troubled themselves over him. Rather than the pampered youngest, he was that other archetype, the youngest who is ignored. But he had one brother whom he loved fiercely, Henry, an actor who, Southwell told Holyoake, had once played Romeo at Drury Lane. Henry it probably was who offered his youngest brother a home after their father's death, but Southwell, sensing that his youthful pursuit of pleasure would be curtailed by such an arrangement, and despite knowing that such brought little lasting happiness, he turned the offer down. The end of the relationship came when Henry died in the West Indies. Charles was devastated when he heard the news: 'I stood motionless for some moments – nor do I think that all the pangs my flesh has been heir to before or since could, if aggregated, equal that *one* then felt'.[9]

---

* Timothy Dwight, Professor of Sacred Literature at Yale College, Newhaven.

His unfixed affections were won by a woman of great attractions, Mary Seaford, who according to Southwell's memoirs, proved to be a 'jilt' within a week of their marriage. Southwell left his wife and was soon receiving the attentions of one of her aunts, 'a fascinating woman of thirty-two'. They met for some time until the aunt declared she could visit no longer unless they married. 'This, for a man already blessed with one wife was a home thrust', Southwell recalls. 'But though not over scrupulous about marriage vows, which my wife had been the first to break, I had insuperable objections to being tried for bigamy'.[10]

Southwell must have possessed certain attractions of his own, enough for the aunt to agree to live with him without marriage, an arrangement certain to destroy the reputation she wished to preserve. They co-habited for six months until Southwell heard of his wife's distress, which he took to be over him but might have been due to an illness she was suffering at the time. He went to see her, and finding her prostrate, and in his emotionally volatile manner, all resolve 'never again to live with her… deserted me, and burying my face in her pillow, I burst into tears'.[11]

Southwell was, then, a highly emotional man, one who snatches decisions from the air and does not form them from much calculation. Here lay the great difference between Holyoake and Southwell. Holyoake later wrote: 'He… in extremens by miscalculation is to be respected – he who errs from not calculating at all is disentitled to respect'.[12] This fundamental difference in thinking would eventually cause a rift between them and leave Southwell the loser.

The relationship with his wife was never happy and the same dissatisfaction marked other aspects of his life. Growing increasingly disillusioned with everything around him, he wrote: 'the scales fallen from my eyes, I did not see men as trees walking, but men as fools acting… No sooner did I reason myself into contempt of organized religion than I began to suspect "there must be something wrong" in our system of Government'.[13] At the time of the Tolpuddle Martyrs affair in 1834, when six Dorsetshire farmworkers were transported for seven years for making an oath of allegiance to the Labourers' Union*. Southwell

* When it was pointed out, first in Bentham's *Westminster Review* and subsequently to the House of Commons, that the Orange Order demanded their members made a secret vow of allegiance, and that Order's Imperial Grand Master, the Duke of Cumberland, brother to the present king, was therefore in a comparable position with regards to the law as that of the six Dorsetshire labourers, their return to England was secured in 1836.

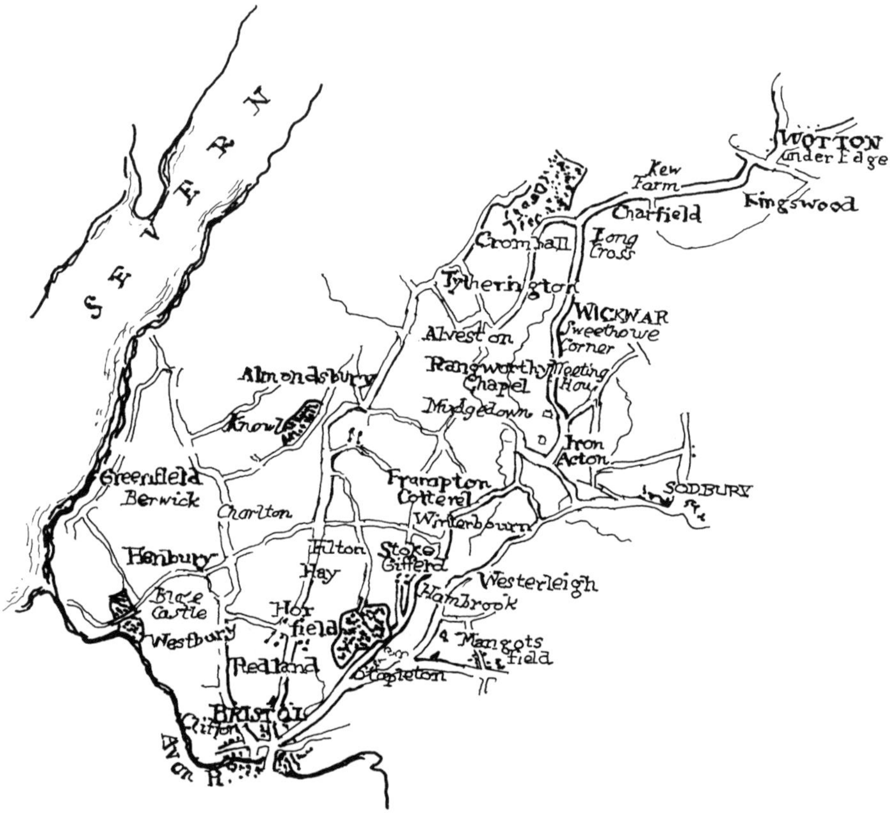
SEVERN
WOTTON
Under Edge
Kew
Farm
Charfield
Kingswood
Cromhall
Long
Cross
Tytherington
WICKWAR
Sweethowe
Corner
Alveston
Rangworthy
Chapel
Meeting
Hou
Mudgedown
Almondsbury
Knowle
Iron
Acton
Greenfield
Berwick
Charlton
Frampton
Cotterel
SODBURY
Winterbourn
Henbury
Filton
Hay
Stoke
Gifford
Westerleigh
Hambrook
Blaze
Castle
Westbury
Hor
field
Mangots
field
Redland
Stapleton
BRISTOL
Clifton
Avon R.

started out in business on Stretton Ground, Westminster, as a bookseller of radical publications. But his wife again fell ill and Southwell, smothered also by the presence of her two dependent sisters, fled the house and went into private lodgings. By now his actions were of a man who walks on irrevocably shaky foundations. He would explain to Holyoake:

> I have felt strongly the passion… of love satisfied and jealous, accepted and repulsed, but my friendship for men generally… has been stronger or at least more durable than my love for women.[14]

Had he chosen a woman with the independence, determination and loyalty of some, like Jane Carlile or Ellen Holyoake, he might have fared better.

Southwell's interest in politics grew. He made his first speech, which addressed ecclesiastical attacks upon the free press, and found that he had a talent for oratory even though his technique was to 'begin without knowing what you are going to say, and end without knowing what you have said'.[15] Holyoake thought him a speaker 'of dramatic power, familiar with the stage as well as the platform'. As he grew older, he was no more inclined to prepare for public speeches than he had been as a young man. Holyoake recalls, when they were together in Edinburgh long after the events dealt with here were safely past, how Southwell spoke for an hour and a half for the benefit of prisoners on a subject which he never touched upon, delighting his audience nonetheless with his wit and vivacity.

Mary Southwell died in 1835. One of her dying wishes was that a surgeon open her up to ensure she was, indeed, dead, and that her heart be removed and used as an anatomical specimen. Her widower witnessed this operation, an event which caused a near riot in the street, after which he was free again to pursue life as he chose. It was at the time of the Carlist infractions in Spain so Southwell joined the British Legion and prepared to fight for the infant Spanish Queen*. With a total absence of pretension bordering on the sardonic, a characteristic which his writing often displays, he explains why he made this decision:

---

* Spain's king, Ferdinand the Great, died in September 1833 having ensured the legality of his daughter Isabella's accession to the Spanish throne. Don Carlos's claim to the throne brought about The Seven Years War, viewed as a struggle between liberalism represented by Isabella and her mother, and reaction represented by the Carlists.

> Many people think I went to Spain solely activated by a noble desire to combat on the side of liberty, but they are deceived. I joined the Legion with the hope of bettering my condition, through some lucky accident, or some bold *coup de main.* [16]

His company departed in that 'crazy old hulk, the *Lord Lyndoch*', from the Isle of Dogs on the 24th of July, 1835, not to return for a full two years in which time he found he did not enjoy war and was, on occasion, more inclined to kill himself than 'strange others'. The time he spent in the army hospital in Vittoria was especially terrible. Admitted with fever, he and his fellow patients had to suffer lice, vermin, cold, overcrowding, dirt, hunger and neglect by the soldiers who ran the place and 'cared only for their own pleasures'.[17] When, finally, he returned to England which before departure he had felt a dislike of due, he admits, to a feeling 'intimately associated with mortified vanity and disappointed ambition', the relief was so great that London, seen from Westminster Bridge and for the first time in two years, 'was [all] *couleur de rose*'.[18] This rose tinted view also took in Millbank Penitentiary, then under the control of the Reverend Danial Nihil who would keep a seven-year-old girl in solitary confinement for twelve months, also two ten-year-olds.[19]

Sadly for him, within two weeks Southwell was back again working for Broadwoods. But in his free time, he attended various debating societies and, through open-air speeches on Kennington Common, became known for his erudition. At this time his interest lay mainly in the denigration of theology. Upon meeting Frederick Hollick, Holyoake's friend from his Mechanics' Institution days, who was creating 'some stir by the delivery of some lectures in the metropolis', Southwell was asked by the committee of the Lambeth Owenite branch to stand in for Hollick as a lecturer for one evening. Ever humorous, Southwell recalls how the committee 'convinced me that Charles Southwell was a cleverer fellow than he ever before had suspected himself to be' and accepted the task at very short notice and without any clear knowledge of the subject, which was "The Production and Distribution of Wealth".

> It was a capital lecture no doubt; for everybody applauded it... so highly did the relieved committee appreciate my exertions on that interesting occasion, that I was forthwith requested again to astonish the natives by my eloquence. I did so, and soon found myself ranked amongst the great sons of Socialism. [20]

The Lambeth Owenites offered him a permanent position and he took it, no doubt feeling that at last here was something he enjoyed and was good at. Late in 1839 he and Richard Carlile met in Lambeth to discuss publicly the fundamental points of Robert Owen's philosophy. Carlile was not an admirer of the system. He believed character to be the work of the individual, not some malleable thing formed from external design. So far as Carlile was concerned happiness resulted from a virtuous life, misery followed from vice. This conviction came from his observation of life, it was not a religious one.

Within a short time of these events Southwell, now a fully-fledged social missionary, arrived in Birmingham and his acquaintance with Holyoake was set to take place. When they did meet, Southwell 'had great versatility... infinite animation, chivalry and daring' Holyoake recalls. Chivalry and daring, instinct and spontaneity were what attracted the careful, almost pedantic young Holyoake. In return, Southwell admired Holyoake's steadfastness. For this mutual respect to have existed between them, both must have sensed in the other the essential ingredient of integrity. Southwell certainly possessed conviction but had a great capacity for offending people and for a quick turn-about in his perception of things; a characteristic which seems to have been caused, for the most part, by disappointment in others. It was a trait which leaves behind it an impression, not entirely fair, of fickleness and unreliability. As it was, the younger Holyoake was prepared to accompany the ex-Legionnaire into dangerous waters.

During these same months, Southwell also encountered for the first time John Brindley who sabotaged the meetings of a lecture tour he made through Yorkshire in the first months of 1840. Brindley was a Cambridgeshire schoolteacher who had taken up a secondary career as declaimer against all things socialistic. A man of rigid religious convictions, he challenged the socialists at every opportunity, tending to trail them and disrupt their meetings when he could. A year after Southwell's confrontation with him, Brindley persuaded Robert Owen to agree to a three day debate at the Amphitheatre at Bristol when he took the opportunity to make a personal attack on Owen, calling his family life and his socialist principals immoral and ungodly. Owen brushed it off, but the *New Moral World* carried letters pleading with him not to subject himself to this kind of attack again. Even before the Bristol meetings Charles Southwell had written:

> It is not fitting that Mr. O. who has seen the snows of seventy winters, should be degraded by the presence and opposition of such a moral

> pestilence as Brindley, whose slippery conduct is now so well known and appreciated, that we cannot meet him without soiling ourselves. [21]

Southwell had a clear perspective of John Brindley and commented that he 'does our cause much good;... he is useful *in spite of himself*; for though he may annoy, he cannot injure us'. He would have cause to reconsider that statement eighteen months later when Brindley's Bristol magistrate friends came for him in the dead of night. But for now all was well, and by the time of the Owenite Congress of 1841 he and George Jacob Holyoake had become good friends.

11

The 1841 Congress of Robert Owen's Rational Religionist Society was held at the Great Hall of the Social Institution in Manchester during a May of poor weather. Some delegates were late arriving and proceedings were adjourned until the second day when Robert Owen took his presidential chair on the platform. Names were called by Walter Newall the Secretary, and minutes and correspondence read, before business began. Charles Southwell was there representing Birmingham.[1]

This congress of 1841 was to prove to be a watershed event in the fortunes of The Society of Rational Religionists. The mind of the now elderly Robert Owen was still focused on cooperative communities despite the lessons of the disastrous attempt at New Harmony in America. As a consequence, the Society of Rational Religionists was committed to huge financial outlay in the building and maintenance of the Queenswood home colony in West Tytherley, Hertfordshire. A grand house had been built there, and this, with general running costs, was largely responsible for the Society's dire financial position in 1841. As the meeting proceeded, Mr Hunt, from the London branch, expressed concern at his branch's drop in income over the last twelve months, from £755 to £427, even though membership was up.

Some delegates were beginning to realize that their president's preoccupation with the establishment of home colonies was unrealistic. They were disappointed at the lack of progress in their more practical social ambitions: "People are quite tired with only lecturing and talking about the thing," John Finch of Liverpool told Congress, "they want to see something done, and there would immediately be a great accession from the Liverpool district".

Joseph Smith, delegate from Huddersfield was 'desirous that all proceedings be of a more energetic character'. "Luke-warmness" he told Congress, "is occasioned solely on account of the lecturers themselves. We need less metaphysics and more downright practical measures for bringing them out of the poverty, wretchedness and misery in which they are placed".

Frustration over the Central Board's policies gathered strength during the first days of Congress while the Board's Annual Report almost entirely concerns itself with progress at the Queenswood community. Due to its perilous financial situation, the number of residents in the colony had been reduced by two-thirds over the past twelve months, but the situation was now improved and the Board hopeful of better times to come. One enthusiastic visitor to the community that year had found it a 'thriving place, well-kept, prosperous', but Queenswood would be declared bankrupt four years later, in 1845.[2] Robert Owen's aim to create socialistic communities so that he might conclusively demonstrate to the world the pre-eminence of his social philosophy, clashed with the desire of members of the Rational Religionist Society to make small improvements which would be felt on the street, in their houses and workplaces. Socialism meant different things to different people.

The key question of education also was a contentious issue by the time of this Congress. Charles Southwell, a relatively recent member of the Society, complained of the cost of schooling, which at Queenswood was seven shillings a week per student, "the charges are too high for the working classes to afford", he said. "There are branch members capable and willing to give [cheaper] tuition and I hope Congress will make a declaration that it should be one of our first undertakings to provide such a school". But Owen felt 'quite sure that under present circumstances it could *not* be effected', although everyone was interested in education and would do all they could to advance it.

Celebration of Robert Owen's seventieth birthday was held on Friday the fourteenth, the fourth day of Congress. He appeared 'in excellent health and spirits' and delivered a short address from the platform, saying how pleased he was to see so many friends before him. John Finch spoke briefly on Owen's 'philanthropic career, high principles, and great benefits to the society'. The weekend came and went, the celebratory mood soon forgotten, Congress reassembled on the Monday morning of May 17th. More expressions of concern over the financial prospects for the society were heard from the floor – the message from the platform was that investors in the Home Colonies must be kept happy while the town missionaries were to keep the philosophical flame alive, presumably on thin air. 'I ventured to suggest', Southwell recalls, 'that, instead of wasting time on chimerical subjects, we should employ it in considering how to deal with tangible and really useful questions'.

Southwell's enthusiasm for the system was already showing signs of breakdown. He declared to Congress his belief that Mr. Owen's policies were the 'dreams of dreamy minded men' and that action aimed towards helping people living in the real world was needed. At this Owen rose and, dismissively waving his hand (petulantly Southwell thought), said that he, not Southwell, was the practical man, that 'the time for agitating the public mind was passed, and the golden age about to begin'.[3] Much had changed since the day twenty-five years previously when, at the London Tavern, Robert Owen had shaken society to its roots by daring to call all religions gross errors. Younger men were coming up, though none more combative than Southwell who, having made his point, characteristically was about to take it too far.

He appealed to the assembly: "As the actions of the Central Board have been called into question, I consider it desirable that any member of Congress should make a perfect *expose* of any acts that he might deem to be wrong", but it seems no-one did.[4]

There was another issue which was to take centre stage in the months to come and which was touched upon at this 1841 Congress. The society had been calling itself The Society of Rational Religionists for two years now and was, certain logic dictated, a religious society, entitled to the protection and privileges afforded to all other religious institutions, and in particular the unhindered collection of funds at socialist Sunday meetings. The one problem with this scheme was that in order to benefit from these advantages the Society's social missionaries must agree to certify and register their offices as places of worship and must, themselves, take a dissenting minister's oath. Southwell said he would rather drop dead on the platform than take the oath of a dissenting minister.

This policy was the last straw for Southwell and Holyoake. Both men took it for what it was, an expedient by which the Central Board hoped to escape further persecutions like that of the Bishop of Exeter's twelve months earlier. Oath taking was reluctantly accepted by many of the Society's members. Lloyd Jones, who straightaway after Congress engaged John Brindley in a debate at Birmingham, was one of the first to take the oath, seeing the great inconvenience that would result to his branch members if he did not, and believing 'one part of the Bible to be literally true, another figuratively'. He had felt justified to do it, 'but was not well pleased'.[5]

A less prominent Owenite, John Perry of Cheltenham, a teacher, also took the oath. He had 'expressed social sentiments in a poem he had published' and, Holyoake says, was warned by the worthies of Cheltenham that 'unless he retracted them he would lose his teachership'.[6] Once the deed was done, 'he was treated with contempt by those who intimidated him. They first destroyed his moral influence, and then despised him'.[7] Perry was dismissed from his teaching post all the same.

The Owenite Board's expediency in pursuing a registration policy dealt a severe blow to the regard in which Holyoake and Southwell held the Society of Rational Religionists. The education question was frustrating enough, and the way in which Robert Owen had 'evaded, not met' the Bishop of Exeter's attack of the previous year still rankled: 'A noble opportunity, such as bigotry seldom affords to a rising party, had been suffered to pass away unused... The enemy triumphed', Holyoake later wrote.[8] The suggestion that he should take the oath of a dissenting religious minister was the end.

Charles Southwell felt the same. He wrote that rather than a Society of Rational Religionists:

> You are fast dwindling into a community of pedlars, with souls so slavish as to think of nothing but driving a hard bargain in the national sale of human industry... Your party is now held together rather by its interests than its principles.[9]

Southwell was so disgusted that he resigned his position as social missionary to set-up his own newspaper, *The Oracle of Reason* in rivalry to Owen's *The New Moral World.* The infamous 'Jew Book' article was written, published and he was in prison within a few weeks. 'I fear I am *in* for it now', he wrote to Holyoake shortly after his trial 'No head in a hornet's nest was ever better stung'.[10]

By March 1842, the financial position of the Rational Religionists was such that its Secretary, Walter Newell, warned all social missionaries that they might be laid off. Holyoake, already infuriated by the society's abandonment of Southwell, did not wait for Newell's notice and resigned his position in early spring, but not before he told his Sheffield members how, during the previous two years:

> the wet blanket of orthodoxy has been drawn round the shoulders of Socialism, and it seems to have stood shivering between Christianity and Infidelity, with too much honesty to adopt the one, and too much expediency to own the other. [11]

Such were his feelings in the spring of 1842, and it is at this point that he and this narrative meet, and where we first meet him walking to Bristol to see Charles Southwell.

12

Also in May 1842 occurred two nationally significant events. One was the publication of Ashley's report into the Employment and Conditions of Children in Mines and Manufacturies. It described, amongst other terrible things, the state of a six-year old girl who was found dragging a half hundredweight of coal. Her wage might typically have been about two shillings and sixpence for a week of this unimaginable work. Children and women worked as drawers of coal, 'with a girdle bound round their waists, attached to a chain which passed under their legs and was fastened to the cart'. This arrangement was particularly uncomfortable if 'you were in the family way', one woman explained. They pulled loads through seams 'not more than a yard in height', sometimes less than two feet. 'Girls from seven to twenty-one worked naked to the waist beside adult colliers who were perfectly naked'.[1]

These were the finer details which Henry Phillpotts' correspondent from Wallsend colliery had had the delicacy not to mention when telling his bishop of conditions in the mines in 1812.

And in May, together with mill and other industry workers, men and women of the mines were beginning to call for strike action against the owners who were seeking to cut wages. There were reports coming from Birmingham that the rate of pay for workmen in the fancy steel toy trade had been reduced by half, and that of workers in the plating trade by at least a third, while the effects of the Corn Laws continued to make life intolerably hard for every one of them. In January, John Angell James had made the unprecedented move of preaching politics from his pulpit when he addressed his congregation on the iniquities of the Corn Laws. He publicly supported a petition demanding its repeal, signed by thousands and which was presented to the House of Commons in the following month.

The country was in a highly volatile mood by mid-1842. In the counties north of Warwickshire, leadership of the organising rebel workers was a critical issue which the Chartists did not hesitate to address by calling for union of action. In contrast to this, the Owenites, at their Congress, this time held at Queenswood itself, in Hertfordshire, were preoccupied with their own problems and still talking about oath taking. Holyoake and Southwell were not there to hear it. They were together at Bristol.

For two days the visitor to Bristol remained unaware that his lecture on Home Colonization had prompted Cheltenham's magistrates to seek his arrest for felony. A notice was posted to him at an address in Eugene Street, Bristol, but the first he knew of his situation was when he opened the *Cheltenham Chronicle's* May 26th issue. Ignoring front page advertisements for medicines for stomach complaints, scrofula, nervous disorders (to which ladies were particularly subject), and ointments for whiter teeth, he would find, on the third page, fourth column, the following report:

> ATHEISM AND BLASPHEMY – On Tuesday evening last a person named Holyoake, from Manchester [*sic*], delivered a lecture on Socialism (or, as it has been more appropriately termed Devilism,) at the Mechanics' Institution. After attacking the Church of England and religion generally for a considerable time, he said he was open to any question that might be put to him. A teetotaller named Maitland then got up, and said the lecturer had been talking a good deal about our duty to man, but he omitted to mention our duty towards God, and he would be glad to know if there were any chapels in the community? The Socialist then replied that he professed no religion at all, and thought they were too poor to have any. He did not believe there was such a being as a God, and impiously remarked that *if there was* he would have the deity served the same as government treated the subalterns, by placing him upon half-pay! With many similar blasphemous and awful remarks, which we cannot sully our columns by repeating, the poor misguided wretch continued to address the audience. To their lasting shame, be it spoken, a considerable portion of the company applauded the miscreant during the time he was giving utterance to these profane opinions.
>
> (We have three persons in our employ who are ready to verify on oath to the correctness of the above statements. We therefore hope the authority will not suffer the matter to rest here, but that some steps will immediately be taken to prevent any further publicity of such diabolical sentiments).

Holyoake was outraged: 'miscreant', 'poor misguided wretch'. This, and another article in which he is described as 'Holyoake the Blasphemous Socialist Lecturer, *monster of pernicious doctrines*', was exactly the kind of defamatory attack to which his sense of dignity was particularly susceptible and which he was incapable of leaving unanswered. Whether with Southwell's and Chilton's encouragement or independently, he decided to return to Cheltenham.

His decision to return immediately to Cheltenham, taken together with events which would take place at his eventual trial, are interpreted by many Holyoake biographers as the acts of a martyr. It was interpreted so by some at the time. A friend from Sheffield, a Christian called Paul Rogers, wrote to him on the 9th of June saying, "you know that I... regret that you should have felt it necessary to *offer yourself as a martyr* in such a cause. For the sake of your health – your comfort – your friends – your amiable wife – your interesting children – consider if there be not a better way of removing the wall of obstruction to what you deem the spread of truth, than the *breaking your own head against it.*"[2] Martyrdom, Holyoake says, never was to his taste: 'No person could be more disinclined than myself to acquire that unpleasant distinction'.[3] But he does admit to 'quite a distinct passion of hatred where I was wronged'.[4] He certainly was impelled by a need, which he could not control, to seek redress for any wrong done to him. The return to Cheltenham was made so he might challenge what had been written in the *Chronicle*: 'If I had been conscious of guilt or had been guilty of any offence which the laws hold or ought to hold as a crime, should I have returned? You may judge from this', he says, 'that I considered I had done nothing of which I ought to be ashamed'.[5]

He was impelled by an egotism which he was well aware was his failing. A pleasure in vengeance, to which he freely admits, had always possessed him and now it overwhelmed even a concern for his family. With the benefit of having spent time with Southwell in his prison cell, Holyoake must have known that his own arrest was certain if he returned to Cheltenham to face his accusers. Ellen and their two infant daughters remained to be provided for, yet he retraced his steps to Cheltenham under a blazing summer sun expressly to stand by what he had said in answer to Mr. Maitland's question at the end of his last lecture, and to defend his right to do so.

On Wednesday, 1st of June, a very hot day, he set out on foot for the town which by now he reckoned would 'furnish a jury who would, under direction, bring in any man guilty of blasphemy who boiled his tea-kettle on a Sunday'.[6] It was already planned that he would speak again the next night at the

Mechanics' Institution, this time on 'Civil & Religious Liberty'. He was offered a bed by his friends, George and Harriet Adams, who sold radical publications, including *The Oracle*, from their house in King Street, and there he stayed, quietly, during the following day so as not to let the authorities know of his presence. That evening, when the time came to go to the lecture hall, he took care not to be noticed entering the place, slipping in 'like sleep' he says, in case he was seen and arrested before he could speak. The Chartist group who had leased the hall on Albion Street for that evening was taking risks too in allowing Holyoake the opportunity. There was only a scattering of people there when he arrived but soon the hall began to fill. The significance of Holyoake's presence would be lost to no one.

He began his speech and, no doubt with the Reverend Francis Close in mind for none in the town escaped his influence, Holyoake said: "After all we have heard about religion with numerous parsons with which you abound… is there not something rotten at the bottom of all this when uttering a few sentences can so shake the foundation on which they are built?". Then, as he saw a number of policemen come into the hall: "They come not forward to refute me but send the police to apprehend me… That is the evil of religion, against which I lift my voice".[7] This was a grave moment for the young social agitator. The policemen stood patiently at either side of the doorway, their glazed hats forming a 'brilliant, but a dubious back ground for a meeting on Free-Discussion', Holyoake recalled.[8]

He addressed the audience for an hour, and when the meeting was over Mr. Russell the police officer in charge came up to make his arrest. "Let me see your warrant", said Holyoake. "I don't have one", Russell replied. Holyoake protested that this was irregular. Others joined in the argument but the policeman would not back down.

Eventually, close to midnight, Holyoake agreed to walk down to the police station. Arm in arm with a friend, probably George Adams, he made his way through the night streets of Cheltenham, along Albion and Winchcombe Streets, then out on to the well-lit High Street, close to Francis Close's Church of St. Mary's, which must have loomed large to the passing prisoner's eye, and left into St George's Place. A walk of only a few minutes, during which the escorting law officers sociably followed on behind.

At the police station he was put into a cell. The twenty-five-year-old Holyoake had come to a place where notable others had been before him: Richard Carlile, Henry Hetherington, John Collins (whose hand he had held as a small boy when they walked the fields to chapel together), William Lovett,

William Cobbett who, in the year of Holyoake's birth, had fled from prosecution to America and had brought Thomas Paine's bones back to England on his return. It must have felt a bit like fate.

The next morning he was taken to the magistrates' court on the High Street, close to St. Mary's Church, where he noted with some bitterness that one of the examining panel was a church minister, one Dr. Newell. The experiences of Charles Southwell at the hands of the Bristol magistrates must have hung, chimera-like, before his eyes as he stood before the bench, but he had the presence of mind to bring out pencil and paper and prepare to take notes. Other personalities at the scene were Mr. Overbury, magistrate; Mr. Capper, magistrate, who ever after remained in Holyoake's memory as a 'vulgar' and 'brutal' old man; one John Lovesey and Mr. Bubb, solicitor. The court was filled with interested onlookers, many of them friends of Holyoake, who heard him charged with having publicly delivered, on the 24th of May, atheistical and blasphemous sentiments. James Bartram and friend were brought in as witnesses to the fact, and Mr. Bubb, solicitor for the prosecution who is described by Holyoake as 'a particularly gross and furious man' stated his position:

"I attend to prefer the charge of blasphemy… Any person who denies the existence of providence of God is guilty of blasphemy, and the law has annexed to that offence imprisonment, corporal punishment, and fine. I shall give evidence of the fact, and I shall ask that he be committed for trial, or required to find bail for his appearance. The offence is much aggravated", said Mr. Bubb, "by his having put forth a placard, announcing a lecture on a subject completely innocent and, having got together a number of persons, has given utterance to those sentiments which are an insult to God and man, and a crime according to the law of the land".[9]

Holyoake queried the legality of his arrest which had been made without warrant to which the elderly Mr. Capper replied that in his case anyone would be justified in taking him up without the authority of a warrant. Holyoake's reply was that other towns of greater bigotry were accustomed to observe this legal formality, by which the tone of the proceedings was set.

"We refuse to hold an argument with a man professing the abominable principle of denying the existence of a Supreme Being", Mr. Capper said and, to Holyoake's deep chagrin, added to this, "Even the heathens acknowledge the existence of a Deity. If you entertain the same pernicious opinion on your death-bed you will be a bold man indeed. But you are only actuated by a love of notoriety".[10]

Holyoake's lack of religion was of little consequence to Mr. Overbury, "but your attempt to propagate the infamous sentiment that there is no God, is calculated to produce disorder and confusion, and is a breach of the peace".

Bail was set at £100 with two sureties of £50 each, a substantial sum which Holyoake could not meet. He had friends in the room, Mr. Partridge and Henry Fry, who promised to stand as sureties, but the Reverend Dr. Newell, having knowledge of Mr. Fry, put an obstacle in the way of this arrangement by stating that Fry was 'not worth £50 when all his debts were paid'.

Bail was refused. At the end of the proceedings Holyoake was taken from the Public Office where the magistrates' court was held, and escorted back to the police-house at St. George's Place where more of the same awaited him. Gloucestershire's superintendent of police, Thomas Lefroy, who had set up the force three years earlier, was there to greet Holyoake, along with police surgeon Mr. Pinching.

Pinching was interested to know whether or not Holyoake believed in Christ, and began 'a dry, historical argument to prove that there was the same evidence for the existence of Jesus Christ as that of Henry the Fourth'.[11] Holyoake pointed out that proof of existence was not the point but the *ethics* of the thing, at which Pinching became agitated.

"Is it not Robert Owen who has made you an atheist?" he asked.

"Mr. Owen himself is not an atheist", Holyoake replied, and explained how the circumstances surrounding Southwell's imprisonment had made him think more deeply about the matter and which had finally ended his belief in the God of churches. Pinching seems to have expected something different from this. He began an animated speech which Holyoake asked him to stop. "Unless you talk with me on equal terms I won't answer you", he said. Lefroy laughed at this and told Pinching he was not being quite fair which had a negative effect on the surgeon. "I am only sorry the day is gone by when we could send you and Owen of Lanark to the stake instead of to Gloucester gaol", Pinching said, and so the conversation ended.

Holyoake says he was then shut up in a filthy place with a lousy man. The building of Cheltenham's policehouse had been completed only in January of that year so it was the case either that the building works had not incorporated a new gaol-house or the cell was perhaps not so filthy as Holyoake remembers it. Handcuffs were placed on him which were too small for his wrists, and eventually these were replaced.

By the afternoon of this first day of captivity it was decided to take him to Gloucester and keep him over there, where Quarter Sessions would be held.

The weather was sultry, Holyoake had walked thirty miles from Bristol to Cheltenham two days earlier, had had next to no sleep since the day before, and his escort now told him he must walk, bound, the nine miles, westward, to the county town. It was a lucky thing for him that the railway had reached Cheltenham the year before and that he had friends in the town to give the sixpences necessary to pay for his and his police escorts' train fares. The station had been situated a mile-and-a-half out of town, so still he had to walk that distance, handcuffed. He was beginning to appreciate the experience of arrest as physically painful and mentally degrading.

Unsure whether or not to take his belongings with him, he decided he would when assured nothing would be taken from him at the other end. Things did not turn out this way as on his arrival at Gloucester his pockets were searched and his papers confiscated.

There were two gaols in Gloucester, one on Southgate Street, complete with tread wheel installed in 1816, the other on Castle Lane, and it is to the latter that the tired Holyoake was taken, late on the 3rd of June. A substantial construction designed along the lines advocated by penal reformer John Howard, the gaol was sited where the old castle of Gloucester once had stood and abutted the muddy banks of the Severn, close to the quay. Its buildings, completed in 1791, were formed around three quadrangles, each three stories high with balconies running the length of the middle and top levels and which overlooked a central exercise yard.

Holyoake, after being obliged to walk handcuffed through Gloucester city from the railway station, would be taken in through the relatively new gatehouse built in the north-east part of the prison wall facing Castle Lane. Now the reality of his situation rushed in on him. Sensations of suffocation came over him when he was put into a cell. He became feverish, a reaction not helped by the state of the bed. Too filthy for him to lie on, he sat on its side in the dark of that night.

The next morning the turnkey, Mr. Ogden, escorted him to the gaol's general room where he was joined by four or five other prisoners all keen to know what he was in for. "We always tells one another", one said when Holyoake kept silent, so he told them 'blasphemy' which none seemed to know the meaning of, and assumed he must be religious. Prison Calendars show that of these companions, one was awaiting trial for stealing two bundles of willows, another for stealing two loaves of bread, two more for the theft of two ducks and a drake. Seeing he was tired and dispirited, they offered him mint tea.

Anxious to prepare for his defence, Holyoake asked for his books from Robert Cooper, the prison chaplain, and eventually one of the Bristol magistrates brought the pencil notes he had made at the examination at Cheltenham and some private papers, but withheld other papers because, he said, they 'were not necessary' to the defence. Holyoake then made out a list of the books he thought he would need for that purpose but a proportion of them was not allowed by Cooper on the grounds that they were of an unchristian character.

However, he was allowed to stay on the Queen's evidence side of the prison where he could be alone. The company of his fellow prisoners was not welcome to him. They were, he thought, 'not of an edifying or improving class'.[12] All the cells there were empty, also the adjacent yard, but he could not escape visits from a number of proselytisers in the first days of his imprisonment. One was Samuel Jones, magistrate and retired preacher, he who had returned to Holyoake his notes and papers, also Bransby Cooper, former Member for Gloucester and now senior magistrate. The latter, who also happened to be the father of the prison chaplain, was a man of 'venerable and commanding aspect, generous to a fault in matters of humanity, harsh to a fault in matters of religion'. The two visitors were ushered into Holyoake's cell by the prison governor, Captain Mason, and both men set about making their theological arguments, oblivious to the embarrassment they caused the young captive.

Bransby Cooper urged Holyoake to agree that he was a deist, "You cannot be an *atheist*, you don't look like one". But Holyoake shook his head while feeling 'very unpleasantly' how much he was in their power. He was beginning to see how someone in his position might give in to a desire to please and make compromises. He said he was an atheist whereupon his visitors, 'flew into indignant revulsions and shouted 'a fool! a fool!' till the roof rang'. The governor, Captain Mason, turned away 'with the air of one not caring to be witness of so much rudeness'.[13]

Days passed, and the matter of bail was still not resolved. The friends willing to stand as sureties for him at Cheltenham had been sufficiently intimidated by the magistrates there to withdraw their offers. The Society of Rational Religionists was not prepared to give any help at all. A letter sent from its central office on Pall Mall, written by William Galpin to one of Holyoake's Cheltenham friends, makes things very clear:

> In regard to all your enquiries respecting legality etc they are easily answered by stating you are the weaker party, are acting against the powers

> that be, and have not the funds to buy redress. Under these circumstances men who go forth to fight must see where their strength lies. In my opinion their only strength will be in the excitement and tyranny of their opponents and this Mr H. seems to be having enough of. [14]

Dark days during which Holyoake felt very anxious, but he was not entirely alone in the world. There was Maltus Ryall, at a distance in London but constant and who, to aid Southwell at the time of his arrest, had received subscriptions at George Huggett's Coffee House in North Place, Lambeth. Ryall, together with fellow socialist and free thinker Thomas Paterson, friend of Holyoake from his Sheffield days, was there to help now. Isolated and worried, Holyoake wrote to Ryall: 'I can only scrape together a few books, and whether I shall ever see then *until* I am taken into court I know not'.[15]

He was due to be tried at Quarter Sessions within the month and urgently needed material for his defence. Holyoake would not rely on counsel, he knew no advocate would be able to argue effectively on a point of conscience. In an effort to improve his position, a memorial describing his treatment at the hands of the Cheltenham magistrates was sent by Henry Fry to John Arthur Roebuck who, until losing his seat in the election of 1837, had been Member for Bath. Roebuck was a member of the Philosophical Radicals and founder member of the Utilitarian Society, he was a small man who suffered periodic bouts of illness. The picture John Stuart Mill paints of him is reminiscent of Charles Southwell: 'he had very quick and strong sensibilities', Mill says, he 'wished that his feeling should be deadened rather than quickened'.[16] And like Southwell, Roebuck tended to associate 'the application of subtlety and tact... with political conservatism and moral weakness'.[17]

Two weeks went by until finally, on the 18th of June, friends from Worcester entered into recognizance for him to the sum of £100. Holyoake, though, would not take up the Bible to swear to his own recognizance. "What does it matter how many gods you swear by," Captain Mason asked him, "since you don't appear to believe in any?". Holyoake was freed without taking an oath, a decision in all likelihood made by Bransby Cooper.[18] After sixteen days in Gloucester gaol he had come to regard this gentleman almost with affection: 'One minute he would growl at me like an unchained tiger – the next he would utter some word of real sympathy, such as came from no one else, and at the end of my imprisonment I parted from him with something of regret'.[19]

He did not go directly home after his release from Gloucester gaol. First he went back to Cheltenham where he learned that, six days earlier, his friends

George and Harriet Adams had been arrested for selling an issue of *The Oracle of Reason*, a copy of which had been bought, for one penny, by an agent of the town beadle from their house and soon put into the hands of the solicitor, Mr. Bubb. After a day under arrest, Mrs Adams had been allowed to return to her children, who, in her absence, had been locked up in their house on King Street under magistrates' orders. George Adams, like Holyoake, was now awaiting trial. Holyoake stayed in Cheltenham for one night before finally making his way home. He arrived back in Birmingham on the Sunday, the 19th of June, some weeks later than originally planned.

13

Holyoake made his way to his sister Matilda's house on Windsor Street in Aston, where Ellen and the children were staying. He writes very little about his family but it was a support to him. Although the religious Catherine Holyoake would have mixed feelings about her eldest son's career, mother and son respected and tolerated each other's convictions. A younger brother Austin actively shared his commitment to socialism and freethought.

Ellen, the younger by two years, was as radical as her husband. They first met during a call Holyoake paid to Belcher's Unitarian book-shop on the High Street, where Ellen worked in service for the household. She allowed him to regard her as a likely 'partner in propagandism', and Holyoake soon came to admire her bright and reticent manner in the face of difficulties.[1] They were married at Birmingham's Register Office on the 10th of March, 1839, where William Pare was Registrar. This was in the last weeks of Holyoake's working life as a whitesmith, and his address is recorded as 10, Skinner Street.

Ellen Williams, a farmer's daughter, appears to have been practical and discerning and, not so ready as Holyoake to see the best in others, could more quickly see deception where her husband could not. One winter's morning, in the first months of their marriage, before Holyoake's association with the Owenites and when he was making a scant living as a free-lance teacher, a 'portly, respectable-looking gentleman dressed in drab', enquiring after mathematics lessons, arrived at the door of their house in Sandpits on the edge of town. Ellen was five months pregnant and the income was needed but, as with the arrangement with George Combe eighteen months earlier, Holyoake did not settle terms. The pupil arrived each morning for five days and left after each two-hour session without paying for it. Ellen said the man had no intention to pay, and she was right.

Another week of lessons followed before Holyoake finally summoned up the courage to ask for payment. There was a scene after which the man in drab promptly quit the house, leaving husband and wife furious and impecunious. They wondered if he might be an informer spying on them, then Holyoake took to looking 'in police offices and assize courts, expecting and desiring to catch sight of the rascal at the bar' where he believed he must end up, but was never satisfied.[2]

His sister Caroline married John Hornblower, Holyoake's friend from his Mechanics' Institution days, and another brother-in-law, Edward Nicolls, whom Matilda Holyoake had married in 1839, just a few weeks after her brother's wedding to Ellen, shared the family commitment to the socialist cause. By the time of Holyoake's return from his spell in Gloucester gaol, Edward Nicolls, in his capacity as provincial secretary to the Anti-Persecution Union, was organizing public meetings in Birmingham's Hall of Science, Lawrence Street, on Holyoake's behalf. Holyoake spoke at one a few days after his arrival back home and was loudly cheered by the crowd. The Manchester socialists held a similar benefit at their Hall of Science at Camp Field which was well attended, and at Sheffield Julian Harney raised a subscription of over £4.0.0. which was handed over to Edward Nicolls.[3]

The letter sent to John Arthur Roebuck had received a reply to say that Roebuck was waiting to hear from the Home Secretary. It had already been decided that Holyoake's case should be heard at the Summer Assizes not Quarter Sessions. This gave him more time in which to prepare his defence and, as Quarter Sessions were presided over by local magistrates, a hearing at the Summer Assizes would ensure a judgement free from the influence of the same magistrates who had initiated the prosecution. A Bill recently had been passed to ensure this in cases of speculative opinion. Holyoake believed the Act was a direct result of his own case.

And so the condition of George Jacob Holyoake, obscure social propagandist, was becoming known in high places. He had promised himself, if he survived his stay in Gloucester gaol (he did not always enjoy the best of health), that he would no longer delay his visit to London. He had two pressing reasons for going there, one was that he could co-ordinate plans for his defence with Maltus Ryall and Thomas Paterson of the Anti-Persecution Union, the other was that it would at last satisfy his longing to see the city where many of his radical heroes had played out their parts.

He says he walked most of the way to London, but as he entered the metropolis by way of Woburn Place his arrival, one Saturday evening early in July, took place, at a guess, by train at the grand and recently built Euston railway station. While the Great Hall was still to be built, the Doric arch was in place beside the New Road, as the Euston Road was called. Across the landscape north of the terminus the effects of rail construction were visible to travellers. Dickens describes in *Dombey and Son* the state of Camden Town, through which the Euston line runs, as: 'enormous heaps of earth and clay thrown up' he writes, 'Here a chaos of carts, overthrown and jumbled together, lay topsy-turvy at the bottom of a steep, unnatural hill, there confused treasure of iron soaked and rusted in something that had accidentally become a pond'.

'Chafed and sad', Holyoake says, he walked for the first time through London. He was enthralled by its grimness. 'Its streets, its pride... its very poverty fascinated me'.[4] He fell in love with the city as many do, and never fell out of it. It was 'magical', 'enchantment', in architectural terms still visibly the work of Wren and Adam. The great sprawl had barely begun. Thomas Carlyle's 1840 description of London conjures it: 'Our old wooden Battersea bridge takes me over the river; in ten minutes' swift trotting I am fairly away from the monster and its bricks. All lies behind me like an enormous world-filling *Pfluister*, infinite potters' furnace, sea of smoke, with steeples, domes gilt crosses, high black architecture swimming in it, really beautiful to look at from some knoll-top while the sun shines on it'.[5]

Nash's Regents Park development was newly built, while still to north and west of the park all remained open land, only on its eastern and southern sides, down to Tothill Fields in Westminster, did building cover the private estates of Church Commisioners, Cadogan, Portman and the Crown. Developers were looking west from Thomas Cubbitt's Belgravia development, but only looking, it was still a country walk to reach Hammersmith from Pimlico. A new Houses of Parliament was in the throes of construction, also the British Museum and, in the city, a new Royal Exchange. Before long Lord Nelson's statue would be raised on to its column in Trafalgar Square which, until quite recently, had been the site of the palace's stables. Holyoake would have been impressed with these works-in-hand, especially with an electric clock which kept time in front of the London Polytechnic Institution in Regent Street. With illuminated face, it ran 'by the agency of a galvanic current', and was a wonder to any who saw it.[6]

North and east of the City, brick and mortar stretched from Islington and Hackney as far as the marshes to the fringes of Poplar, where, close by, Marc Brunel was preparing to open for foot passengers his Thames tunnel, connecting Wapping to Rotherhithe. South of the river, which is where Holyoake was heading, the Minet family had already leased building plots along Camberwell New Road west of the Old Kent Road, but in development terms Brixton and Camberwell were virginal Surrey landscape.

Upon arrival, Holyoake walked straight to Lambeth. He had recently spent a number of weeks in towns and cities filled with the sound of seagulls but London was a city of sparrows, its predominant representative of the avian class which flew in great swirling clouds above the streets. Their chirping was a constant accompaniment to the great human noise of the city. He would pass through this unparalleled din before reaching Lambeth, on the south side of the river Thames, and relative quiet again.

Maltus Ryall was there to greet him. This was probably their second meeting (Ryall seems to have been in Birmingham earlier in the year) and it would have been a warm one. Ryall had offered a life line to the young radical during his time in prison and Holyoake must have felt great gratitude towards the older man. There and then, they set about answering correspondence and arranging the order of Holyoake's legal defence. Ryall already had written to Richard Carlile asking him to join in a public debate on Holyoake's behalf. The reply had been cautious. Carlile did not want to 'play second fiddle to any man who has not the same experience and the same standing on the question'.[7] But later he agreed, with the warning that:

> In speaking I should treat of nothing but the common principle and condemn no one but the common enemy of the Priesthood and such like. I want no more quarrel with politicians, but with some that I know, I will not have acquaintance or companionship. [8]

Holyoake's first night in London was spent in company with Ryall in Lambeth, 'in a summer-house, in a garden... Morning had long broken' he recalls 'before we lay down on the benches to sleep'.[9] In consequence of Ryall's approaches, an invitation for tea had arrived from Richard Carlile, and as chance would have it, the following afternoon on a day of brilliant light and fierce heat, Holyoake met him in the street.

> As I was passing Blackfriars Bridge at two o'clock in the afternoon, I saw approaching a short, thick-set gentleman, with piercing eyes and pleasant though resolute expression of countenance... The friend with me stopped and introduced me to Richard Carlile. He greeted me with many friendly words of commendation, which I valued as coming from a veteran prisoner for opinion to one who had scarcely entered the ranks. [10]

Carlile took an immediate liking to Holyoake and asked him to join a discussion which would follow a lecture he was giving that evening on 'The New Scientific Interpretation of the Scripture'.

Carlile's mode of challenging religion had changed over the years. He had come to believe that religious institutions could best be changed from within, that it was a hopeless task to try to change them from a position of militant opposition. The great agitator had taken out a preacher's licence. This put Holyoake in a difficult position. He did not want to offend Carlile whom he greatly admired, but was shocked at the older man's new position in relation to religion. It had been only three or four months since Holyoake had resigned his post as an Owenite missionary because of this very policy which he saw as an expedient with no merit attaching to it.

This night's lecture on 'The New Scientific Interpretation of the Scripture' exemplified Carlile's new approach to the issue which was to ameliorate the effects of superstition and biblical literalism with reason and scientific argument, rather than to challenge them directly. Privately, Holyoake thought Carlile's position a lapse of conviction, but he was, nonetheless, flattered to be part of the event. 'There was no name known to me in London from whom an invitation could have come which I should have thought a greater honour'[11] he later wrote.

He duly turned up at the Hall of Science on the City Road, a building 'constructed in a waggon yard' near the Bunhill Fields Cemetery, where he and Carlile had tea together and shared the first of what would be many talks on defence tactics for Holyoake's forthcoming trial.[12] Carlile would prove to be a useful and loyal friend to Holyoake in the weeks to come.

The evening's lecture would have run along the lines of the articles Carlile published in his *Christian Warrior*:

> The first problem in human or social reform is *through what medium must it be made*. In what is called a religious state of society, that is, a state of idolatry and superstition, can reform be carried out through any other medium than its religion? My experience... is that with a religious people religion is the only medium of reform... Socialism may create twenty Tytherlies, but it has still done nothing for the nation. But science thrown into the Church as a substitute for superstition in the education of the people, begins at once to regenerate the people, the parliament, the institutions, and the throne. [13]

At the finish, Carlile asked Holyoake to give his opinion on the system he had adopted. Holyoake answered that it was the ethical interpretation only which interested him. Anything the Scriptures might contain which was 'consonant with experience and conducive to the public welfare' he accepted on that ground'.[14] The working classes did not have the leisure to study theology and could only have salvation at second hand, but 'moral truth they could have first hand, since it rested on experience, conscience, and common sense'.

* * * * *

Years before, Carlile had gained public notoriety through a tour he made with the lapsed clergyman Robert Taylor when they entered Cambridge in May, 1829, and there, uninvited, challenged various collegiate heads to debate on 'the merits of the Christian religion', their object to put the case for free discussion and social reform.[15] Carlile and Taylor, who knew Cambridge well having studied theology at St. John's College, caused a tremendous stir for five days and, by posting their bills from his house, managed to jeopardise the livelihood of their landlord, Mr. Smith; presumably a sympathiser but also licensed by the university which took a dim view of his involvement.

Judging by his portrait, Carlile had every appearance of a man of genial nature. He possessed a formidably high forehead and a head of soft, waving hair, well-shaped eyes brimful with intelligence, his chin had a slight cleft. He was born in Ashburton, Devonshire in 1790, son of an exciseman who, he says, 'neither cared about wife nor children' and who died before his son was five years old. There was no sign, in his early life, of the radical he would become: 'I was a weed left to pursue its own course' he says.

> In my youth there was nothing singular; as a boy among boys I thought more of excelling them in their foibles than in their virtues... I had some of the works of Paine in my hands before then, but... although I heard them praised, I felt no desire to read them, whether from prejudice or a total lack of ideas upon politics I do not know. [16]

Perhaps the fact that he lived in a society which burned Thomas Paine's effigy in preference to Guy Fawke's each November has some bearing. Some education came his way, first at a dame school run by 'old Cherry Chalk, who taught the alphabet on a horn book, and performed all sort of cures without medicine by the potent power of charms!' 'She was not a witch', he wrote, as '... there was another old woman who had the title of the witch, and one in a town is enough on whom Christian ignorance might vent its spleen'.[17] And before he was taken from school at the age of twelve, he first learned some Latin the acquisition of which, he says, was the source of his first vain thought.

He loved and admired his mother who kept a shop. Thinking it was the best thing for her son, she insisted on his seven years' apprenticeship to a tin-plate worker in Exeter, but it was a business he did not like and his time at it was so much misery to him for, having been spared the predations of his father, he fell into the hands of this other cruel man, who 'cared no further about me than as to the largest quantity of labour he could obtain from me upon the smallest quantity of food'. The youngster was treated like a slave and teased by his playmates for it. Before the end of his apprenticeship he seems to have exacted some kind of moral revenge for he says in his memoirs:

> I taught that master... that mine is a temperament from which persecution can wring nothing but perseverance in resisting it, and that neither pains nor poverty can subdue me, where I see myself to be right; and even if in error, a good word, a soft word will do in a moment that which no menace or punishment will ever do. [18]

After a false-start, he established himself in London as a journeyman mechanic to Matthews & Masterson, in Union Court, off the Holborn Hill. These were restless times. As the Napoleonic Wars ended, domestic unrest began. By 1817 the market was flooded with desperate and hungry men unable to find work, and London saw meetings and rioting in Spa Fields. 'In the manufacturies' Carlile remembers, 'nothing was talked of but revolution'. High bread prices were the cause of much of it. The spectre of the French Revolution still danced in the minds of the ruling classes, and the authorities clamped down on all acts of malcontent, even signs of it, by the people, and the young Carlile saw just how nervous London's radical tract sellers had become to distribute anything for fear of prosecution. Even the fearless William Cobbett abandoned his *Political Register* which astonished Carlile as he thought the *Register* 'mere milk and water' in comparison with other publications.

In the months before Holyoake's birth, Carlile began to understand the nature of political and social repression and the importance of a free press. It came to him quite suddenly when he was twenty-seven years old, like a conversion.

> I soon became so far fired as to begin to build castles in the air. I attended the public meetings, and felt an attachment to Henry Hunt as what I

> thought the best and boldest man... [and] as well as to read I began to scribble. I annoyed the editors of several papers with my effusion... but every answer was that it was too strong or violent. [19]

Parliamentary reformer Henry Hunt and his friend William Cobbett struck the young Richard Carlile with awe. He submitted copy to them, at one time pacing in front of Hunt's hotel in Covent Garden for two hours, bursting to hand him a letter and dreading its receipt in case he was 'called before him!'.[20] On March 9th, 1817, Carlile borrowed one pound from his employer and purchased with it one hundred copies of Wooler's *The Black Dwarf*, which he distributed to retailers, well aware that in doing so he was likely to fall foul of the authorities. When the paper's publisher was arrested Carlile, keen to take his place, offered to act as his stand-in but was not taken up on the idea. Then, in April, the printer William Sherwin offered Carlile the publishing of his paper, *Sherwin's Political Register*, and run of his shop at 183 Fleet Street.

Carlile had found his element. Sherwin and he shared views and styles – a certain violence of writing 'calculated to keep up the other political writings to something near the standard'; this at a time when desperate handloom weavers and spinners from Manchester marched on London, while the government, also desperate in its way, banned public meetings and suspended the Act of Habeas Corpus.[21] No one was as willing as Carlile to publish and distribute articles guaranteed to bring the weight of the law down upon them. Henry Hunt now sought him out, visiting him at Fleet Street to commend his bravery.

This was the very time at which Robert Owen decided to make his speech against all religions at the London Tavern, but Carlile missed the event because, one week before, on August 14th, he followed in his hero Hunt's footsteps and was sent to the King's Bench Prison for publishing Mr. Hone's religious parodies. Owen had been invited to attend Carlile's trial but being too taken up with his own affairs, the 14th of August being the date of the first of the two London Tavern meetings, he could not be there.

This was the first spell of many years of imprisonment for Carlile. In the course of his life he spent nine years, seven months and one week in prison in the cause of a free press. These were years he seems to have enjoyed, the manner of one's imprisonment then being, to some extent, something you fashioned for yourself to be as comfortable as you could afford. Always supported by campaigners on the outside, he seems to have found the constraints of prison life peaceful and calming, an environment where he could study and write. This peculiar trait meant that he was quite fearless of punishment which made him a difficult case for the authorities, and this was just as well because he was bound, some time later, to come up against the Blasphemous and Seditious Libel Act of 1819.

This was a repressive Act under which Stamp Laws were applied to the radical penny issues, purposely to take them beyond the purchasing power of the poor and disaffected, while swingeing fines were imposed upon defiant presses. Some thought parliament and not laws controlling the press should be reformed. With this view in mind, Henry Hunt agreed to be the main speaker at a public meeting, called by the Manchester Patriotic Union Society, which was to assemble in St. Peter's Field, outside Manchester, on the 16th of August, 1819. Carlile, now a name in his own right, travelled up for the event. Reports suggest that some thirty thousand people were there for that day's meeting, men, women and children, many turned out in their Sunday best. It was a meeting which local magistrates had attempted to ban and who had taken the precaution of ordering the removal of stones from St. Peter's Field which might be used as weapons against the authorities.

At twenty minutes past one o'clock the speakers arrived at the enclosed field. Hunt, a big man with a booming voice, stood upon a wagon, surrounded by banners, and started his address when, according to Carlile:

> A cart, which evidently took its direction from that part of the field where the police and magistrates were assembled in a house, was moved through the middle of the field... [and] had no sooner made its way through, than the Yeomanry Cavalry made their appearance from the same quarter as the cart had gone out.

In fact the police, ordered by the Manchester magistrates who were convinced that there was danger of insurrection, had refused to go into the field to arrest the speakers without the back-up of the soldiers. And so the local yeomanry, made up of farmers, mill owners and their sons, in other words the employing class of the area, went into the crowd. They galloped round the field and, Carlile reports:

> after a moment's pause, they received the cheers of the police as a signal for attack... The Yeomanry Cavalry made their charge with the most infuriate frenzy; they cut down women and children indiscriminately... The police were as expert in applying their clubs to the heads and

> shoulders of the people as the cavalry their sabres... One woman, who was near the spot where I stood and who held an infant in her arms, was sabred over the head, and her tender offspring drenched in its mother's blood. Another was actually stabbed in the neck with the point of the sabre... Some were sabred in the breast – so inhuman and fiendlike was the conduct of the Manchester cavalry. [22]

At least eleven people were killed, and some hundreds grievously injured by sabre cuts and beatings. Henry Hunt was eventually arrested.

From Durham, Henry Phillpotts defended the action of the yeomanry and eruditely opposed calls for an enquiry into the behaviour of the Manchester authorities. He put his name to a declaration in which the signatories declared 'that we... defend, to the utmost of our power, the altars of our God, the throne of our King, and the glorious free constitution of the country'.[23] The Prince Regent wrote to thank the Manchester authorities for their prompt action. In London, the less illustrious Richard Carlile who had managed to escape the field and arrest, wrote an open letter to the Home Secretary calling for Manchester's magistrates to be brought to justice for 'the unprovoked slaughter of the peaceable and distressed inhabitants of that place...':

> in the event of the Government failing to give satisfaction to the full extent of their means... the people, not only of Manchester, but of the whole country, are in duty bound and by the law of Nature imperatively called upon to provide themselves against the attacks of similar assassins acting in the true Castlereaghan fashion. [24]

He also wrote in similar vein to the Prince Regent. For his pains, Carlile, already waiting upon proceedings brought against him for republishing Thomas Paine's *The Age of Reason* and Palmer's *Principles of Nature*, spent six days in the Giltspur Street Compter on a charge of sedition. Persecution being publicity, sedition being catching, the authorities promised him bail if he would agree to withdraw his letters from circulation but, summoning the character he had honed as an apprentice, this he refused to do. He considered prison a more honourable fate than freedom to walk on the streets at the discretion of his opponents.

As the charges relating to his publication of Paine's and Palmer's books were still pending, he was indicted under these charges for blasphemy, while the inflammatory letters relating to the Manchester massacre were left to be forgotten by a restless public. Carlile had to answer separate charges for both books and after defending himself (and while he was at it reading out the whole of *The Age of Reason* to the court) the judge gave him a three years' prison sentence and imposed a fine of £1,500. He made a bow to the assembly in the Guildhall where the trial took place, was handcuffed, and taken away to Dorchester gaol.

14

On the Monday evening of 18th July, 1842, Holyoake made his way to the House of Commons to hear Sir James Graham, Secretary of State, speak on the circumstances surrounding his arrest at Cheltenham. Charles Barry's and Augustus Pugin's gothic Houses of Parliament was still some way off completion and the House assembled in the Court of Requests in the old, fire damaged building. If Holyoake came there from Lambeth he would have crossed the Thames over the stone bridge, the old Westminster bridge, on which Charles Southwell had stood the day he returned from his two years' fighting in Spain, with its fifteen circular arches, their piers each topped with a domed octagonal recess built to give shelter to pedestrians from inclement weather but which also provided good hideaways for robbers during dark hours. It was a light summer evening when Holyoake crossed.

Sitting with companions, he listened to the Secretary of State speak in his defence. Serious irregularities had been committed by the Cheltenham magistrates in their proceedings against George Jacob Holyoake. They had treated their prisoner with unnecessary harshness and had acted without legal warrant. It was all refuted by Craven Berkeley, member for Cheltenham who, in 1834 had pressed for mitigation of the Tolpuddle Martyrs' sentences. His brother, Grantley Berkeley, as it turns out, would be foreman of the grand jury at Holyoake's coming trial. According to the *Cheltenham Free Press* Grantley Berkeley was an absentee planter of the West Indies, who argued for the replacement of Negro workers with Irish and European emigrants because the Negroes, "will only work for wages amounting to an inordinate bribe, their love of gold is not sufficient to induce them to work for fair and moderate gain".[1]

When the speeches relating to his trial were over, Holyoake stayed on at the Court of Requests to listen to the address of a young, dark haired man, who, one of his companions told him, went by the name of William Ewart Gladstone. In years to come, Holyoake would correspond with Gladstone.

Heartened by this visit to the Commons he wrote to Ellen four days later, on the 22nd of the July, from Thomas Paterson's bookshop in Holywell Street just up from the Strand, to say he had seen various lawyers. Holyoake's defence hung on the principle of free speech: that every man had the right to 'promulgate his opinions upon every subject without incurring civil penalty', and the legal view, he told his wife, was that his trial would result, at worst, in a short imprisonment and possibly none at all.[2] He also wanted to check that money promised by the Anti-Persecution Union for the children and Ellen's subsistence had been paid at Birmingham's Post Office. 'I shall be at Home on Monday night' he wrote. 'I attend at the Globe Coffee House, Holborn tonight. Tomorrow I am to open a discussion... On Sunday morning to Lecture at the Rotunda, and in the evening at John Street'.[3]

Imagine his feelings. Within a few weeks he had found himself famous, the centre of activity, sought after by personalities whom he thought venerable and way above and beyond the comings and goings of his modest life. His delight in these connections never diminished. Many years later he recalled: 'How sweetly... came the notice the *Weekly Dispatch* gave me of my first lecture in London... To succeed in any way in London was more than I ventured to expect'.[4]

To lecture at the Rotunda in 1842 was as great an event to a young socialist and propagandist as to play the O2 at Greenwich is to a performer today – both are the venues of great acts which have gone before. The Rotunda, once a famous music hall where Samuel Taylor Coleridge had lectured on Shakespeare, and Hazlitt on the *English Comic Writers*, had been reopened in May 1830 by Richard Carlile and Robert Taylor as a meeting place for social reformers and radicals. The building stood in Great Surrey Street, now Blackfriars Road, and it was here that Taylor, dubbed The Devil's Chaplain, gave his astronomico-theological orations and mocked Christianity in a manner that makes Southwell's attempts sound tame. It was soon closed again, when, in November of that year and in an atmosphere of violent malcontent due to lack of food supplies to the working classes, the government had the building surrounded by troops to prevent meetings.

Two years later, the year of the Great Reform Act, Carlile's indomitable common-law wife Eliza Sharples reopened the building. Her husband was undergoing a spell of imprisonment, this time at the Giltspur Street Compter. Almost immediately the Rotunda became the main venue for the reformists Henry Hunt and William Cobbett who addressed vast crowds on the subject of parliamentary reform, calling for votes for every man.

The historical importance of the Rotunda was keenly appreciated by George Jacob Holyoake on his first visit to London, and he felt it to be a great occasion the day he lectured there to a full and enthusiastic audience on The Right of Free Discussion. Soon it was time for him to return to Birmingham, and before he left London it was arranged that the editor of the *Daily News*, Mr. Knight Hunt, author of 'Fourth Estate' and son of Leigh Hunt, would travel to Gloucester to report on the trial to be held there. The date for it was drawing near and Holyoake first wanted to spend some time with his family. He carried with him to Birmingham some books which he had picked up for Ellen and, returning via Wolverton where he gave a lecture, arrived home on Monday, 25th of July.[5] Maybe he had a small gift for each of his daughters too. Madeline was now two years old, her sister, Eveline just seven months.

Only eight, nine days at most, remained to him before he must make his appearance at Gloucester. Difficult days for Ellen, not quite of the organizational mainstream of her husband's defence, with two infants to care for and scant supply of basic needs. The time came for him to leave for Gloucester. It was a bright afternoon when he set out on his final journey that year. Holyoake could make no provision for his family beyond a weekly ten shillings promised by the Anti-Persecution Union, and that was not guaranteed. His final parting from his family must have been difficult. Ellen kept the elder child to her lap in an attempt to distract her, but when Holyoake finally left the house and was half way down the street, he heard the sound of Madeline's voice calling after him. He turned round. She had followed him out on to the street and he saw her black eyes gleaming. He says she shouted out to him, "Dada, You won't be coming back!", which was the child's prescience. He never did meet her glance again, or hear her voice any more.[6]

* * * * *

The 1842 Summer Assizes opened in Gloucester on the 6th of August. Holyoake arrived, in good time, in the city where Henry Phillpotts had spent his childhood sharing the diminished fortunes of his father, the late proprietor of The Bell on Barton Street. Phillpott's brother John was now Member for Gloucester, and living comfortably in Brunswick Square.

The city had undergone much redevelopment in recent years. The streets, cleared of the old wooden buildings and other obstructions, were now paved and lighted. Pin making was Gloucester's main manufacture and the port, fed by the Severn and the Berkeley and Gloucester canal, was busy, so it did not much matter that the city's pump room and its saline spring was less fashionable than Cheltenham's spas. In the last ten years its population had increased significantly and now stood at nearly sixteen thousand.

Holyoake stayed at The Ten Bells public house on Westgate Street during the days before his trial where he received a number of visitors. He says his room quickly became 'like a Convention'.[7] Richard Carlile had arrived in Cheltenham some days before and, coming on to Gloucester, remained with Holyoake for the duration of the Assizes. Knight Hunt joined them, and Henry Fry from Cheltenham who was supposed to have brought Holyoake wine and birds from a Mrs. Chichester of Gloucestershire* but who ate and drank everything himself except for a small bottle of raspberry vinegar.

Holyoake applied to the court for a copy of the indictment, but found it too expensive to buy at eight shillings and six pence. 'The jurors for our lady the queen, upon their oath', the indictment read:

> present that GEORGE JACOB HOLYOAKE, late of the parish of Cheltenham, in the county of Gloucester, labourer, being a wicked malicious and evil-disposed person, and disregarding the laws and religion of the realm, and wickedly and profanely devising and intending to bring Almighty God, the holy scriptures, and the Christian religion into disbelief and contempt among the people of this kingdom... with force and arms... in the presence and hearing of divers liege subjects of our lady the queen, maliciously, unlawfully, and wickedly did compose, speak, utter, pronounce, and publish with a loud voice... these words following, that is to say, "I (meaning the said George Jacob Holyoake) do not believe there is such a thing as a god, I... would have the Deity served as they (meaning the government of this kingdom) serve the subalterns, place him (meaning Almighty God) on half-pay" – to the high displeasure of Almighty God, to the great scandal and reproach of the Christian religion in open violation of the laws of this kingdom, to the evil example of all others in the like case offending, and against the peace of our lady the queen her crown and dignity. [8]

He did, however, purchase a copy of that week's *Cheltenham Chronicle* for it carried a report of the grand jury proceedings which he had attended. The

* Could this be the same Mrs. Chichester who, in 1846, advised a depressed Henry James Snr, when visiting a spa town, that he was suffering from what Swedenborg called a *vastation*? (Wilson 1999, p.314).

grand jury's job was to examine the prosecutor's evidence and determine whether it was sufficient to go to trial. The *Chronicle* said that the judge assigned to the case had connected Holyoake with publication of the *Oracle of Reason*, a fact for which he was not indicted. The *Chronicle* also reports the judge to have described Holyoake's words on the night of the Cheltenham lecture as a folly deserving of punishment if it could be proved they were said with the intention of offending.[9] "When I saw his lordship", Holyoake later recalled, "surrounded by the learned counsel, heard him deliver his charge in the midst of the array of talent then present... I then thought, as I do now, that such persons could surely have found nobler means than the employment of brute force to negative anything I could do, should I ever attempt – which I never had done – to bring anything truly sacred into contempt".[10]

The judge in question, Thomas Erskine, was the grandson of the lawyer who had defended Thomas Paine's right to publish the second part of *Rights of Man* in 1792, and a man considered to be patient and fair-minded. Holyoake's plan to defend himself would mean long speeches and hours added to the court's time, so Erskine arranged to hear his case last. There was, then, a full week in which Holyoake could fine tune his defence and go about in the sunshine in Gloucester rather as a tourist. He was recognised on the streets, and was stared at a great deal. 'I am quite well' he wrote to Ellen after a few days there, 'and in first rate spirits', despite being:

> a little disappointed at not being tried by this time but it gives me more time for sleep and pleasure so I do not much care. I am sure to have some imprisonment so do not be surprised should you hear this result, I do not expect much... [A] Great many persons say they shall come to see me when in prison if I do go there – so I shall have company at times. Supped with Mr & Mrs Partridge on Sunday. Both come to the trial. Kiss Made[line] for me... Your very dear, George. [11]

Much of this week he spent as a spectator in the court room. 'If ignorance would look upon its own degradation, let it spend a few hours in an assize court' he later wrote. The fine-looking Shire Hall, built on Westgate Street twenty-five years before with its tall Ionic portico for an entrance, held the Assizes in specially built semi-circular courtrooms at the rear of the building. A variety of cases were heard that week, more than one committed by Mr. Overbury, the Cheltenham magistrate who had presided over Holyoake's appearance back in June.

Holyoake sat and watched the proceedings. Sarah Gibbs, for stealing sixty yards of nets, was transported for ten years; a seventeen-year-old, John Troughton, for stealing Eliza Evans' silver spoon, transportation for seven years; and on the third day, William Garroway, his right arm tattooed with the figure of a woman, had to answer to charges of verbal assault, the theft of a purse containing coins, also a silver watch, four sovereigns and a head of mutton.[12]

Almost certainly it was this man whose crime, Holyoake thought 'indeed arose out of depravity, but the depravity arose out of bad training and vicious circumstances'. He describes how the offender: 'was sentenced to transportation for life to Norfolk Island, the most ferocious sentence an English judge can pronounce'. When Garroway heard his fate, he bowed in genuine and awkward humbleness, and said, as he made a rustic bow to the bench '*Thank'ee, my Lord!*'.[13] Holyoake was deeply shocked at the humiliation of this middle-aged man who 'had been taught to bow to his pastors and masters, and… bowed alike when cursed as when blessed'.

It was a short walk from the Ten Bells, on Westgate Street, to Gloucester Cathedral. Holyoake relates to Ellen in a letter (which survives today despite being damaged or half eaten by Madeline) that he entered the cathedral on the Sunday morning to hear the sermon but 'was not converted'.[14] As he was a conspicuous figure in the city and was to be tried the very next day for blasphemy it was a bold thing to do. He asked after his 'sweet little girls', sent his love to Madeline and hoped that they were all in good health.

At ten o'clock the next morning he had a breakfast of three beaten eggs, and then, accompanied by Richard Carlile, presented himself at the Shire Hall. It was good theatre that George Adams' trial was to be held on the same day, also useful to the prosecutor, who could see the benefit to him of linking Holyoake with Adams' indictment for selling copies of the *Oracle of Reason*. The courtroom was full. Its business that day promised entertainment to ladies of fashion, wives of the clergy, interested gentlemen and members of the local landed gentry. The press was well represented.

George Adams was called first. His defence was conducted by Mr. Thomson, a barrister whom Holyoake, watching on, says, 'began by sympathising with all the disgust invented by the counsel who opened the prosecution, and… ended by expressing Adam's sorrow and contrition for what he had done'.[15] Mr. Adams, however, did not feel any contrition and said as much. The jury found him guilty.

'George Adams,' Justice Erskine began, 'you have been convicted of the offence of publishing a blasphemous libel, and the libel which was proved to have been published by you was one of a most horrid and shocking character… Although by the law of this country every man has a right to express his sentiment in decent language, he has no business to make use of such shocking language as this… you have expressed, through your counsel, contrition… But if you ever offend again, it will then be known that you are determined to persevere, and it will be seen whether the law is not strong enough to prevent it. The sentence of the court is, that you be imprisoned in the Common Gaol of this county for one calendar month'.[16]

Here is a stark and strange discrepancy between this and the sentences given to the common criminals, so-called, of the previous week who fall right out of the bottom of Disraeli's Two Nations concept. Even men of Holyoake's stamp were inclined to dismiss this underclass as not deserving much sympathy.

What length of sentence could George Jacob Holyoake look forward to? As he stood waiting to be called his mind must have focused like an actor's on the performance ahead. The many preceding weeks' activities and discussions on argument, the advice given by Carlile whose own trial twenty-three years earlier had been full of man's right to free thought and expression and the consequences of state protection of religious institutions on the working classes, all had arrived at its climax and Holyoake must carry it forward. Although such a young man, he was familiar with public speaking and had formulated good practice.

He knew not to drop his voice at the end of a sentence, and that over abundant gesturing would turn an audience against him. Passion of conviction was a prerequisite to any good speech, but Holyoake was wise enough not to try to synthesize it, as he knew nothing would be more likely to lose an orator his following than that he display an 'intensity' which is not well founded. 'Those who distrust your judgment cease to be under your influence'.[17] He was careful of emphasis and tone. But he did truly dread losing his voice, that weak and reedy voice, and anticipated indistinctness and 'alternations of screechings and whisperings'[18] if it should fail to hold for the duration of his defence address. When finally he was called into court he carried with him a bottle of raspberry vinegar given to him by Carlile as a reviving spirit for the vocal chords, and which no doubt acted as a mental and emotional strengthening too. Also in a pocket of his jacket was a small portion of tobacco and a letter from the Society of Rational Religionists on the back of which he subsequently made notes.

Mr. Ogden the turnkey of Gloucester gaol and whom Holyoake describes as 'a tall, stout, surly, imperious, pock-marked person'[19] directed him to the bar but Holyoake wanted first to sort his books and papers. A corded chest containing these had been carried into the court for him and now stood on the floor by the dock. Holyoake asked Mr.Ogden to pass it to him. "You can't have that box here", was Ogden's reply, "Go to the bar and plead". Holyoake insisted that Mr. Ogden hand up the box. Suddenly feeling his conspicuousness in front of a watching courtroom, Ogden gave in and handed up the box. A small victory. The defendant asked Justice Erskine for the use of a table and was offered a boarded ledge behind the bar. Holyoake spent some twenty minutes arranging his books and papers to his liking on this ledge, and only then did he go forward to make his plea of not guilty.

Upon the reading of the indictment, which in describing Holyoake as a labourer, a 'wicked malicious and evil-disposed person' replicates the one made against Richard Carlile in 1819, the trial of George Jacob Holyoake began.[20] The first thing Holyoake did was to object to the jury member John Lovesey, the same John Lovesey who had sat on the bench at Cheltenham. 'He is not disinterested in this matter' Holyoake told Judge Erskine. Erskine thought this, 'not sufficient reason for challenging', but after further discussion suggested to John Lovesey that it was 'as well to go', which he did.

The young Holyoake displayed considerable presence of mind throughout his trial which, in his view, was about the right to free speech. The prosecution's focus was on the charge of blasphemy: to prove that the defendant had deliberately set out to ridicule God. Mr. Alexander, prosecuting, explained to the jury that the prisoner was indicted not for writing but for *speaking* blasphemous words, and that although the accused is not the vendor of the *Oracle of Reason*, he supposes him to be the *author* of 'what was made the subject of the last prosecution' – at which point Erskine cuts him off: "You must not proceed in that way. You must not assume". [21]

"I was only going to draw the attention of the gentlemen of the jury to the coincidence of the words". Alexander replies. He goes on to charge Holyoake with a 'horrible' blasphemy premeditatedly committed under the pretence of giving a lecture on Home Colonization. James Bartram of the *Cheltenham Chronicle* was then called to give his evidence.

Holyoake, convinced of behind-the-scenes involvement in his arrest of Cheltenham's parish vicar Francis Close, now asked Bartram why he thought the words he had heard spoken at Cheltenham were blasphemous. "Because they revile the majesty of heaven, law and order," the printer replied, "and are punishable by human law, because they attack human authority". At Cheltenham's magistrates court Bartram had not been so erudite on the subject.

"Who has instructed you to define blasphemy?" Holyoake asked.

"I have not been instructed, it is my own opinion", the printer said, and went on to deny, at Holyoake's questioning, that he had spoken to any clergyman on the subject since May, or that he knew the parties who had got up the prosecution. He also denied that his job was in jeopardy if he did not appear as witness for the prosecution. Holyoake wanted to know if the witness thought he had spoken against morality at the lecture. Bartram thought not. Holyoake accused Bartram of acting as an informer. "It is irrelevant", Erskine said. And following the prosecution's brief re-examination of the witness Holyoake expressed surprise that he had heard 'nothing, not one word, to prove the charge in the indictment'. 'There has been adduced no evidence to show I have uttered words *maliciously* and *wickedly* blasphemous. I submit to your lordship that there is not sufficient evidence'. Erskine said it was for the jury to decide and that now was the time for Holyoake to defend himself.

If he was nervous it did not show. He refuted the accusation that he had secretly planned to speak about religion on the night at Cheltenham, his subject had been colonization and he had merely responded to an unexpected question from one in the audience. Perhaps Mr. Maitland's question had been a form of entrapment; perhaps this, not his answer, had been planned in advance of the lecture? If this were so, the jury should consider whose plan it was. When Holyoake, much later, brings up the name of Francis Close, it is to quote from a printed speech made by the clergyman on the damaging effects of education on Christian adherence. Close, a respected educationalist, was not alone in fearing the consequences of knowledge for the masses without religious controls. The promulgation of Christianity was widely regarded by the respectable classes as a prerequisite to proper education.

Holyoake's defence revolved around certain major topics of concern to radical minds at the time: church establishment, the impropriety of juridical and ecclesiastical connections, the nature of Christianity and the nature of blasphemy, all of which hung upon the issue of free speech. Of the first, he brought up the matter of the previous week's grand jury deliberations, and produced his copy of the *Cheltenham Chronicle* in which Judge Erskine's apparently prejudicial comments were printed.

Arguing that he should not be in the dock at all, 'standing in a place appropriated to felons, to defend matters of a speculative nature…', he said to the jury:

> You who usually have to punish *dishonesty*, are now called upon to punish *honesty* – for hypocrisy and lying would have saved me from this charge. I

> have infringed no law, injured no man's reputation, taken no man's property, attacked no man's person, broken no promise, violated no oath, encouraged no evil, taught no immorality – set only the example of telling the truth... I only expressed an opinion... What can we think of the morality of a law which requires secret inquiry which prohibits the *free* publication of opinion? [22]

Justice Erskine reminded him that the law allowed the expression of opinion if given 'seriously and decently', then 'all men are at liberty' to say what they please.

Holyoake thought this did not correlate with his experience. "Whatever the law says, if an informer can carry the words to parties interested in the suppression – if policemen can be sent to apprehend without warrants the man who publicly expresses his opinions – if he can be handcuffed like a felon and thrust into a gaol – if indictments can be brought against him, and he be put to ruinous expenses and harassing anxieties... then I say the law is a hollow mockery, and its exercise a shameful farce".

He goes on to defend the cause of socialism and suggests that he is as much in the dock for being its supporter as for the charge of blasphemy, and uses the moment to expound socialism's principles which would 'suggest a means of affording employment and thus mitigate the crime which judges and juries are called to punish'. More's 'Utopia' is quoted, also passages from Paine, Southey and the Reformation protestant Peronnet Thompson. He uses the persecution of Galileo just as Carlile had in 1819. He also mentions his infant sister's death as a cause of his religious doubts: 'Gentlemen, will you wonder if, after this, I doubted a little the utility of church establishments?'.[23]

Of blasphemy he says: "threats of damnation and cries of *blasphemy* have always been rife when priests have thought their power and privileges in danger that which mortals cannot comprehend, it is impossible they can bring into contempt... In this case, the supposition is, that God is blasphemed by my integrity in telling the truth".[24] Of Christianity and free speech: "I was never vain enough to wish my views should become universal. All I ask is liberty to express my opinions... If I were a Christian I might spread my opinion far and wide, but because I differ they are declared improper".[25]

"Christ was to me a pattern of meekness and kindness" Holyoake tells the court, "and if I had been asked then if he would have persecuted anybody, I should have given it the most indignant denial. I little thought I should have received such treatment from the followers of the same Jesus".[26]

He was speaking well and his voice had held. It was now four o'clock in the afternoon and Holyoake's address so far had lasted five hours. The jury asked for a short break. When they returned he resumed his argument on the logic and justification of the reply he had made to Mr. Maitland's question at Cheltenham.

"My having stated that I disbelieved in the existence of a deity makes it plain that I could not have referred to a being who was a nonentity in my esteem... I spoke of the heavy expense of religion, and it is to that and that alone I referred... I have lived all my life among those classes who suffer from the burthen of poverty, and I find by a calculation that has never been disputed, that the English pay five times as much for their religion... than any other nation".

It is now that Justice Erskine gives Holyoake an unequivocal opportunity for escape. "If you can convince the jury that your only meaning was that the incomes of the clergy ought to be reduce", he says to him, "and that you did not intend to insult God, I should tell the jury you ought not to be convicted. You need not go into a laboured defence of that".

This is the moment when, ever after, George Jacob Holyoake would be branded as a martyr. His return to Cheltenham after his first lecture had been, to his mind, an act of honour, his time in London had produced support from prominent men and women, many people had spent long hours advising him how best to proceed, giving weight to the idea that the injustice which had been perpetrated should be addressed, that he represented a cause which must be pursued. The human investment in his appearance this day had been huge, and its planners, promoters and audience expected great things. Many of his friends were in court to give their moral support. Richard Carlile, one of the greatest social agitators of the age was standing close by to help and to administer to his needs, Knight Hunt was sitting quietly as he transcribed proceedings. How could Erskine's offer of easy acquittal be accepted with all this weight of expectation upon him, and how could he walk away from an unrepeatable opportunity to state his case?

With barely a pause he replies to Justice Erskine: "It was stated by one of the witnesses at Cheltenham that I said Christians are worshippers of Mammon. I thought it necessary to refer to it... Had it been necessary I could have proved... that I was justified in saying so". He picks up, maybe Carlile passes to him, two copies of the Bible which, he claims, contain passages far worse than anything he had said. Too terrible, he says, to allow him to quote them, ladies being in the room. And so he proceeded for a further four hours, giving as he went a thorough exposition on common law in relation to his case, arguing that he had no case to answer. In fact, Hale's seventeenth century dictum, stating that Christianity is part of the law of England, was not successfully challenged until 1883 by Lord Chief Justice Coleridge in a case of blasphemy against Ramsay and Foote.

Just before nine o'clock in the evening Holyoake drew his speech to a close. "A great principle is involved in the decision now to be arrived at", he told the court, and turning to Justice Erskine asked him to see beyond the 'vulgar prejudices of fanaticism':

> I believe that in every honest heart there is a sense of rectitude that rises superior to creeds, that respects all virtue and protects all truth, that asks for no names and seeks no precedents before resolving to do rightly. That fears no man's frowns, and dares to be just without any man's or custom's permit. That ever generously rises the firm friend of the calumniated and deliverer of the oppressed – to this feeling, gentlemen, only do I appeal, and by this verdict I am willing to abide. [27]

And so George Jacob Holyoake concluded his defence. Its main thrust throughout was the defence of freedom of speech, and it had been masterfully delivered by a young and mainly self-taught man. All told, he had spoken for nine hours and fifteen minutes.

* * * * *

Justice Erskine turned his attention to the jury composed of local traders and farmers, men who, Holyoake always maintained, were incapable of following the intricacies of philosophical discussion. With the light outside the courtroom windows now faded, the air inside very stuffy, Erskine began his summing up. The place had remained full all day, and everyone was exhausted, with the exception of Holyoake whose voice not only had held but had increased in strength as the day had passed. He felt ready to go on a further few hours.

"Gentlemen of the jury", Erskine began, "although the lengthened address of the defendant has demanded from you so long endurances... I still trust we shall have enough of power left to direct our minds to the parts of this case which are important... We are not sitting here as a deliberative assembly to consider whether in respect of such cases as this it is politic or wise to imprison for opinions... we have to decide on the law as we find it".

At this point he felt obliged to defend himself against the suggestion that he had prejudged the trial's outcome at the time of the grand jury sitting. "I told them what I feel, that without religion there is no morality".

"I am not going to lay down as law that no man has a right to entertain opinions opposed to the religion of the state, nor to express them... [but] we require that they shall express them reverently, and philosophers who have discussed this subject all agree that this is right... What you have to try", he directed the jury, "is that the defendant wickedly and devisedly did intend to bring the Christian religion into contempt among the people... You are not called upon to say whether in your judgment the opinions of the defendant are right or wrong... but whether he uttered these words with the intent charged in the indictment". However well Holyoake may have argued against the charge, Justice Erskine reminded the jury that under common law, "Any man who treats with contempt the Christian religion is guilty of an indictable misdemeanour". It is, he told the jury, a matter of *intent* – had the accused intended, by using levity, to ridicule God? There was no evidence to suggest he had planned in advance to say what he did say but, Erskine put to the jury, if the words had appeared as a written paper, "you would have entertained no doubt that the person who had uttered these words, had uttered them with levity... If you are convinced that he uttered it with levity, for the purpose of treating with contempt the majesty of the Almighty God, he is guilty of the offence. If you think he made use of these words in the heat of argument without any such intent, you will give him the benefit of the doubt".

Justice Erskine concluded with a warning to the jury not to take 'statements in newspapers, or other statements made out of court, and consider it in reference to the evidence'. [28]

It was now close to ten o'clock at night. The jury deliberated for little more than two minutes before returning a verdict of guilty. Holyoake was sentenced to six months' imprisonment. If he had been charged with, and found guilty of writing blasphemous articles in the *Oracle of Reason*, or if it had been proven that he had premeditatedly said what he did say, the sentence would have been severer. He was convicted of uttering words with improper levity against God.

Richard Carlile was waiting to greet him as a champion as he stepped down from the dock and Holyoake was allowed to walk with George Adams to the gaol where he was put into a night cell. He had eaten nothing since breakfast, and Richard Carlile's raspberry vinegar was all he had had to drink. Now one of the gaolers took an apple from his own pocket, gave it to him, and fetched him a cup of warm water. It was too late at night for anything more.

Holyoake records that he had been prepared to defend his right to free speech and to promote the interests of socialism no matter what the dangers might be to himself.[29] Unlike Richard Carlile he would find imprisonment hard. Carlile earlier had advised him to have his trial delayed if possible to avoid spending the autumn and winter months in prison. Luckily, the weather that winter would not be a repeat of the bitterly cold winter of 1841.

15

The workers' strike of 1842 was at its height in the months of August, when George Jacob Holyoake was tried at Gloucester. When he first set out from Birmingham on the 22nd of May, working men and women were using that same day of rest to meet in fields and on moorland to plan their action. By the time of his trial, the general strike was at its height and during the first few weeks of his imprisonment it was fading into nothing. It is interesting to find no mention in his memoirs of the workers' strike of 1842.

The strike, the first of its kind, was not politically motivated but became so with increasing Chartist involvement. In earlier years there had been riots over lack of food, but this unrest was different despite the fact that people were going hungry. In 1842 it was a strike for restitution of pay and against pay systems. Black Country miners were often paid in goods instead of cash and at irregular intervals. There was a compulsion for many miners and their families to spend what pay they received in public-houses owned by their masters, despite legislation to stop the practice.

In April 1842 the Dudley nail-makers went on strike. A riot ensued which was put down by regular troops, but the strike went on for some weeks. The Chartists pressed harder to establish a concerted effort of Chartist and operative which would bring the government to a point of reform. Their optimism was immense and continued so throughout the summer months despite the disappointment of May.

On the 8th of July the miners on the North Staffordshire coalfield withdrew their labour. This was the start of the Plug Plot which, in practical terms, entailed the raking out of fires and the drawing of plugs from the boilers, simple acts of sabotage which demobilized the pit engines. By the 3rd of August starving, striking miners in Lanarkshire had begun to steal potatoes from nearby fields, and within a few more days men and women at Stalybridge and Ashton had turned-out and were marching on Manchester, where the Chartists welcomed them. The strike movement spread to Lancashire,

Cheshire and the industrial West Riding of Yorkshire, and to Leicestershire and Nottinghamshire, and was regularly recorded in the Chartists' Leeds based paper, *The Northern Star.* By mid-August the government feared general strife and prepared itself for insurrection. In London, hundreds of Chartists gathered on Islington Green while the Prime Minister, Robert Peel, and Home Secretary James Graham held an emergency Cabinet Council meeting at the Foreign Office. Men and artillery were held in readiness at Woolwich for action against local rioters. Similar orders arrived at St. George's Barracks for the Third Battalion of the Grenadier Guards.

The strikers could not sustain their campaign for they depended entirely upon the goodwill of sympathetic shopkeepers and handouts from the better-off to keep them from starvation, and as soon as the shopkeepers and the better-off sniffed political aims in the air, they withdrew their aid. It was the Chartist and Anti-Corn Law elements which triggered this middle-class reaction despite the fact, as one striker put it, that "the men did not follow the chartists for the chartist principle, [they] fled to them for refuge and were glad of anyone to come and instruct them about the prices of iron and so on".[1] The strike of 1842 was a hopeless dream made of desperation, and finally it dealt the Chartists another crushing blow when men and women began to return to their places of work having achieved none of the aims they had set out to obtain.

* * * * *

Also in the August of 1842, and an interesting juxtaposition of events it is, John Angell James was putting into motion a great plan which he had long nurtured. His object, a union of the Protestant churches. 'No thoughtful Christian can be otherwise than afflicted by the multiplied sects, divisions, strifes, and controversies of Christendom', he wrote. 'Strange and mournful it is that the prayer of our Lord for the visible unity of His people should not yet have been answered in any tolerable measure'.[2]

While the country's operatives organized to do away with social injustice, James sought to eradicate spiritual error which he found in all the diverse Protestant institutions of the country. Spiritual and temporal law, being providentially fixed, allowed no scope for intellectual diversity, but what it did provide was absolute truth by which error could be eradicated and souls saved. If Christians organized, the message could much more effectively be taken out to those in need of it. The Congregational Union was the body to do it.

In May, when Holyoake was making his way to Bristol through middle-England and when workers were organizing in their local fields, James was addressing the Annual Assembly of the Congregational Union in London. This was a time when he thought he might be dying and was inclined to move as little as possible from his Edgbaston house, but he attended the Assembly to disburden his heart:

> There is, in spite of the bigotry, prejudice, virulence, and hostility which is manifested in every direction, an under-current flowing, a yearning for more extensive union… It appears to me that we have it in our power to raise up a defence against Infidelity, Popery, Puseyism, and Plymouth-brethrenism, by bringing about a union of all Protestant bodies of Christians holding the Voluntary principle. [3]

After the Assembly, and a few days after Holyoake had delivered his first lecture at Cheltenham, James, safely back in his home, wrote a letter to the Congregational Union in which he formally proposed the formation of a Protestant Evangelical Union, based on the principles of the inspiration of the Holy Scriptures which 'are the sole and sufficient rule of faith in matters of religion' to which every man has the right 'to judge of their meaning, to the exclusion of all authoritative, traditional interpretation', but with the exception of those fundamentals which are the Holy Trinity, the Atonement, salvation by grace and justification by faith alone.[4] It was from this desire for Christian union that the great Evangelical Alliance was born.

There is little doubting John Angell James would hear of Holyoake's activities as events unfolded throughout that summer of 1842, the lecture at Cheltenham, the arrest, the imprisonment; and he would be shocked and saddened to hear how his former pupil was fallen into the abyss of infidelity. Holyoake had once said that he felt prepared to promote the interests of socialism 'though hell itself should gape', and it is certain that, unlike Carlile, he found imprisonment a bit like hell's waiting room.[5]

Despite his recently acquired familiarity with Gloucester gaol, trouble arose on the first morning of his six months' prison sentence after he failed to respond to the chapel bell. Holyoake's place at chapel remaining empty, Robert Cooper sent a turnkey for him. Holyoake was amazed to hear that he was expected to attend a Christian service, and when pressed to go, said, "In that case, you had better get assistance and carry me. I don't think I should like to go".

"You know, Mr Holyoake", Robert Cooper said later that day, "you are in prison, and must do as you are bidden".

Holyoake assured him he was quite aware of his situation: "Still, it doesn't justify me in addressing to heaven words that aren't true. If you will arrange that I come into church at the time when you start to preach, I'm ready to do that".[6]

The chaplain, whose piety Holyoake likened to 'cold water', was noncommittal and did not again insist on his attending prayers or sermon, although Holyoake went of his own accord in time for the following Sunday's sermon in the hope he might hear something new.[7] As to the chaplain's father, Bransby Cooper, Holyoake grew to like him so much that he says he would have undergone conversion had he been able to gratify him. Gruff and dictatorial but fair-minded in his dealings with others, Bransby Cooper inspired respect in Holyoake.

His first welcome visitor at the prison was Richard Carlile, who came bearing provisions and the news he had heard through the foreman that the jury had been in favour of his acquittal but could not get over the denial of a God. Holyoake had already reckoned on the jury's inability to understand the difference between denial of man's idolatry and denial of God. He had claimed to be an atheist to Bransby Cooper in June, but Holyoake always retained a deist's view. 'I never denied a god', he wrote later, 'I could not have said that, because I am not sure of it... disbelief is all I profess'.[8] Carlile also brought praise and encouragement to him on that first day of imprisonment, telling him he had thought his self-defence 'the most splendid of the kind ever delivered in this country'. "I could scarcely restrain myself from jumping into the dock to embrace you on several occasions" he said.[9]

But they had to speak to each other through an iron gate so the young prisoner, humiliated beyond words, hurried the meeting to a close.[10] He was even less prepared for the visits of strange, fashionable people who thought him an intriguing spectacle. An anteroom was provided so he could escape from view.

Twenty miles or so to the south, Charles Southwell was still confined to his Bristol cell, with a further five months of his sentence to serve. His time there had been bearable. Maltus Ryall's Anti-Persecution Union continued to provide funds, some of which he was able to spend on the luxury of ale. Within four days of Holyoake's trial, Southwell had received news of it and responded:

> You seem to have gained golden opinions from all sorts of people that you made the very best appeal for liberty that has yet been heard within closed walls called Courts of Justice... Hope your treatment is good... There is something in integrity, talent and courage that inevitably carves out a passage for those who have them *if they be patient.* [11]

Another problem arose for Holyoake in the form of the prison garb which he was expected to wear. Refusing to allow the prison authorities to lower him to the status of a criminal, he would not put on a criminal's clothing. 'Of course they said they should compel me', he recalls, '… my reply was "it would be necessary to dress me every morning, as I might not like to put the dress on myself". As it was never done, I fancy they thought the trouble of it might be too much for them'.[12]

In a letter written to Ellen at about this time he says that the magistrates were behaving more civilly towards him, that he was cheerful and hopeful. This was a letter of encouragement not entirely reflecting a reality which included the person of Samuel Jones. Reverend Samuel Jones had attended the first hour or two of Holyoake's trial, had departed then come back some hours later thinking it would be all over and Holyoake 'half dead'. Instead he had found, to his astonishment, that the defendant was in full stride, addressing the court 'as fresh as a lark!'[13] Just a few days into his imprisonment, Jones told Holyoake that Richard Carlile was dead, had died 'horribly' and had recanted 'his dreadful principles on his death-bed'.[14] "You will see what you have to look forward to", Jones warned him. Carlile was busy about Gloucestershire at the time, giving lectures as the Reverend Richard Carlile, and visited his young friend soon after this piece of news had been delivered. Holyoake suffered bullying of this kind from a number of visitors and proselytisers.

He met his fellow prisoners in the common room on a regular basis. All were there for petty crimes or acts of violence. Holyoake gave them lessons, but derived no pleasure from their company. Autumn came on and the evenings drew in, and no light was provided in his cell, so he could not read or write for long hours together. To overcome this deprivation he devised a system which involved drawing thread across sheets of paper which he then secured with pins. Writing within the lines of the thread he could, by this method, produce articles and letters in the dark. Some of the cells at Gloucester gaol were in a filthy and verminous state, the pillows were hard enough to flatten and hurt his ears, and there is some suggestion of fever, or typhoid, in the place. It seems his time at Gloucester gaol was harder than for Southwell at Bristol, or Carlile at Dorchester.

Carlile's room at Dorchester had been 'large, light, and airy':

> It had a sink, water-pipe, and complete lavatory attached, the necessary outfit being provided for hot or cold water at pleasure. A sofa was also supplied. Every other consideration was shown as regards the prisoner's

> physical comfort. In this respect, Dorchester gaol was far superior to most of our reformed prisons of to-day, even as regards provisions for the comfort of political prisoners.[15]

Carlile, however, was kept in solitary confinement for a long time, through which he temporarily lost his power of speech, but it did not seem to affect him mentally in any noticeable way. His wife, Jane, joined him in his cell on January 1821 and stayed for two years, during which time they planned their eventual separation. He was always supported by innumerable well-wishers and colleagues.

Holyoake's time in prison twenty years later was not so good. The surgeon appointed by the local magistrates to take care of the prisoners' health was 'timorous' Holyoake says, and lacked the necessary 'resolution or independence to act upon his own judgment when it conflicted with [the] political, theological, or personal prejudices' of his employers. Conditions were notoriously harsh in nearby penitentiaries, and when a Chartist prisoner called Charles Beale died at Northleach Bridewell, a Commission, headed by Dr. Blissett Hawkins, was sent to look into conditions there. The Commissioners visited Gloucester giving Holyoake the opportunity to tell them it was not good enough that 'a prisoner must die before responsibility could be brought home to the surgeon'.[16]

By September Holyoake was not well. "Had much ill health" he wrote in his log book . "A pain in my side prevents me sitting even for a few minutes together". In Birmingham also, things were difficult. Ellen was receiving a little money from disparate sources, but the pressure of the situation seems to have told on her nerves. On a day in October, Madeline, who was sickening at the time, fussed for a bun she had seen in a shop window, Ellen lost her temper and slapped her. Within a few days the two year old was showing signs of serious illness and her chastisement was to become the act of a moment for which the chance of forgiveness was too quickly taken away.

The difficult conditions Holyoake had to contend with in Gloucester gaol did not keep him from writing copious numbers of letters as well as two pamphlets, one entitled *A Short and Easy Method With the Saints*, the other a refutation of Paley's *Natural Theology*, a copy of which had been given to him by a visiting justice in the hopes that it might convince the prisoner of his error. In his *Refutation* Holyoake revisits the idea that the existence and nature of God is too great a question to contemplate. 'If natural theologians were content to stop where they prove a superior something to exist, atheists might be content to stop there too'.[17] For Holyoake, a natural, human sense of morality was far more certain a thing than a religious law based on analogy and creed, and this was the idea he would build on for the future.

While he scribbled away in the dark in his cell in Gloucester gaol, British soldiers were fighting bloody battles in Afghanistan, Hong Kong was about to cede, forever they thought, to Her Britannic Majesty, Spain was poised to experience another *coup d'etat* in the endless troubles concerning the young Queen Isabella. The Irish nationalist Daniel O'Connell was planning his campaign for repeal of the Union of England and Ireland, while in England and Scotland the unprecedented social disturbances which had broken out during the summer had faded away, and over fifteen hundred workers, Chartists, radical booksellers and paper editors had been arrested.

On the 14th of October Holyoake received a letter from a Birmingham friend, Mr. Seymour, telling him that Madeline was ill. 'Your pretty Madeline is *very ill*', his friend wrote. 'I saw Ellen last night, she had been to say that Madeline is *worse* today. I fear you will lose her, and I make you acquainted with her condition that you may not be suddenly surprised if my apprehensions prove correct'. Seymour tells Holyoake how Madeline, missing her father, had said the evening before that her "dadda was coming to see her".[18]

Madeline died two days later, on Monday, the 16th of October. Her father received the news a few days later when Ogden the turnkey brought him the black-edged letter. Holyoake received it in the exercise yard in the company of the governor of the gaol, Captain Mason. He does not describe his feelings. Carlile had also received a letter sealed with black wax during his Dorchester imprisonment and, knowing it carried news of his mother's death, threw it aside for four hours before he had the courage to read its contents. Madeline had died of fever complicated by malnutrition, and Holyoake forever after would think of her as having 'perished'. His last memory of her was when she was 'full of life and glee'.[19]

Preserved in his Log Book is one of the two-year-old's memorial cards, prepared by Mr. Seymour, describing Madeline as 'the interesting and beloved daughter of George Jacob Holyoake'. Equally pathetic is the knowledge that her father was not able to make his own daughter's funeral arrangements himself, or to be there at her burial. The grieving Ellen received his letter some days later, 'My Dear', it began, 'I hope by this time you have become composed and resigned to the loss of poor Madeline'. Ellen travelled from Birmingham to see him a week or two later, bringing their surviving daughter Eveline with her. For this occasion Bransby Cooper made sure the bereaved parents met privately in the magistrates' room, and Holyoake was ever grateful for this small kindness.

Ellen was inconsolable and again he writes to her, towards the end of November, saying, "Do you think that I have forgotten you":

> ... There is a very pleasing sentiment in one of Southwell's letters to me, that I have thought of mentioning to you. Referring to Madeline, he calls sorrow for the dead but "an amiable variety of lunacy" meaning that such grief is madness, but that the affection and good nature which causes it makes it "amiable"... You must try to remember Madeline's beauty and charms as a pleasing dream, and rather be glad that it continued so long, than grieve that its duration was so short. [20]

His letters and memoirs give little more than a stoic's response to the death of his daughter. During these dark months in Gloucester gaol, Holyoake was less assiduously nurtured by his friends and colleagues than he had been before his imprisonment. He did received letters from Maltus Ryall, and one from Charles Southwell when Madeline's death jogged his conscience. Neither had written for some weeks. 'I am almost ashamed of myself' Southwell writes from Bristol on the 26th of October, '*Letters should* have poured in upon you like a deluge but somehow or other I have lately felt a great disinclination for writing. I read prodigiously':

> ... Just a few, very few words about the sorrow you *must* feel for the loss of your little Madeline. The strokes of grief are unavoidable but the loss forever of those we most love are the sharper inflicted by stern fate – since the death of my favourite brother I have not known grief, and firmly believe never shall again. Enough, more than enough of this, what is past cannot be recalled. [21]

Now light was provided for Holyoake in his cell until nine o'clock each evening for the remaining winter months, and the chaplain thought it a good idea to suggest that if he promised to stop his advocacy of socialism a small school could be set up for him and for Ellen. Tempted with a chance of early freedom and certain employment if he would compromise his convictions, Holyoake, needless to say, did not accept the offer.[22]

In the meantime, Richard Carlile had returned to Enfield to pack up the house in which he had lived with Eliza Sharples and their children for many years. With renewed vigour, very possibly produced by the excitement of Holyoake's trial, he and his family were to move back to Fleet Street to live and work. While helping, in wintry weather, to remove belongs from a cart to carry into the new house in Bouverie Street, off Fleet Street, one of his boys roamed off into the city. In a panic of fear for his young son, Carlile went in search of him and subsequently caught a bad cold.

Just down from Fleet Street at Number 8, Holywell Street, north of the Strand, Thomas Paterson was preparing for Christmas, not in any traditional manner but with placards and effigies placed in his bookshop window designed to insult those of the most liberal religious feeling. He had taken up the editorship of the *Oracle of Reason*, and in the absence of Holyoake and Southwell was presently regarded as the leader of this small group of sceptics and atheists. Carlile by this time had been grossly offended by Southwell who had accused him, from his prison cell, of 'gratuitous impertinence' when the former had described Holyoake as a Christian. Carlile had meant that Holyoake's moral fibre bettered many Christians', and that he could, therefore, as well lay claim to the epithet of Christian as any professing the faith.[23] Carlile now wrote to Paterson describing Southwell as a 'low minded blackguard'.[24]

In the depth of Gloucester's winter, a destitute labourer contrived a short prison sentence for himself in the hopes of receiving a decent Christmas dinner courtesy of the prison kitchen, but when his plan was uncovered Robert Cooper and the Reverends Newell and Jones 'abolished Christmas pudding on Christmas Day for all the prisoners there', in fear that the idea might catch on with others in need of a sanctuary.[25]

Punch ran a Christmas poem called 'The Pauper's Christmas Carol'. One stanza went:

> Fed upon the coarsest fare
> Three hundred days and sixty-four
> But for *one* on viands rare,
> Just as if I wasn't poor!
> Ought I not to bless my stars,
> Warden, clerk, and overseer?
> Heighho!
> I hardly know –
> Christmas comes but once a year. [26]

Christmas passed, the new year began and Richard Carlile, who had been ill with bronchitis ever since the frantic search in London's streets for his missing child, carried out his plan to move back to Fleet Street. He had been warned that his health could not be expected to improve if he did not stay out of the city, but on the 7th of January the move took place and he returned to where, years before, he had fearlessly played out his campaign for a free press. At the same time, Thomas Paterson was imprisoned for one month for the offensiveness of his Christmas window display.

Holyoake had one last humiliation to endure before his release from gaol in the new year of 1843. The prison chaplain, Robert Cooper, in a final effort to make some impression, invited him to a private meeting in the prison chapel. Holyoake was not keen to be preached to, and only reluctantly submitted to the arrangement whereby Cooper stood at his reading desk, while he 'the sole member of his congregation in that gloomy chapel' sat in a pew. For all Cooper's effort, Holyoake was implacably resistant to his appeals, and for the simple reason that the chaplain was insensible to the offence he gave Holyoake in treating him as though he were a 'scoundrel', or in some way inferior. If the prison chaplain had only had the good sense to sit side-by-side with Holyoake and talk on equal terms, then at least he might have received some thanks for his effort. As it was, their relationship remained a failure. Holyoake refused the gift of 'a little, squab, dumpling edition' of the Bible, but, he recalls, 'would have accepted a better-looking copy had one been offered'.[27]

His release took place on the 6th of February, 1843, a few days after Southwell's release from Bristol gaol. His regard for Bransby Cooper and the governor, Captain Mason, remained with him for years after, and was one positive memory he would take with him from the place. After spending the first day of his freedom with William Chilton, and as if to wave a stick at the enemy, he proceeded to Cheltenham where he remained one day and night before returning home. He entered the house in Birmingham in time to witness the birth of a child to one of the family. Pure symbolism of renewal after punishment, life after death.

There was one more loss to be suffered before Holyoake could think of the future. Richard Carlile, whose cold had turned badly and who had been unable to speak for some days, died at the age of fifty-eight, at Number One, Bouverie Street, Fleet Street; on 'the battlefield itself', his daughter called it, 'the old ground where for twenty-five years he had waged such a stern fight against tyranny and injustice'.[28] His death took place two days after Holyoake had made it back home. Despite the epithet of 'reverend', Carlile was morally and intellectually consistent to the last. "The enemy with whom I have to grapple is one with whom no peace can be made. Idolatry will not parley. Superstition will not treat or covenant. They must be uprooted for public and individual safety".[29] This he wrote when there were only two weeks of battle left to him to fight. "After all these years of suffering and toil he died," lamented Eliza Sharples, "wanting the necessaries of life. Oh, ye gods! Such being the reward of sincerity, who then shall marvel at its absence".

His biographer reminds us that 'the honour of vindicating the common people's right to knowledge was to be his'. Jane Carlile died in the same house three months later.

16

On the first day of 1843, Lord Greville, musing over the state of the country, wrote in his diary:

> It is curious to look at the sort of subjects which now nearly monopolise general interest and attention. First and foremost there is the Corn Law and the League; the Corn Law, which Charles Villiers... long ago predicted to me would supersede every other topic of interest, and so it undoubtedly has. Then the condition of the people, moral and physical, is uppermost in everybody's mind, the state and management of workhouses and prisons, and the great question of education. The newspapers are full of letters and complaints on these subjects, and people think, talk, and care about them very much. And last, but not least, come the Church questions – the Church of Scotland, the Church of England, the Dissenters, the Puseyites. Great and increasing is the interest felt in all the multifarious grievances or pretensions put forth by any and all the above denominations, and much are men's minds turned to religious subjects. One proof of this may be found in the avidity with which the most remarkable charges of several of the Bishops have been read, the prodigious number of copies of them which have been sold. Of these, the principal are the charges of the Bishops of London (Blomfield), Exeter (Phillpotts), and St David's (Thirlwall), especially the second. This charge, which is very able, contains *inter alia* an attack upon Newman for Tract No. 90, and a most elaborate argument, very powerful, in reply to a judgement delivered by Brougham at the Privy Council in the case of... Lay Baptism. [1]

The Oracle of Reason, which had caused such outrage and had led to the imprisonment of three men, did not last out the coming year. Maltus Ryall and William Chilton kept the paper going from a temporary office at 46, Wych

Street, off the Strand, in the belief that Charles Southwell, when released, would return to its helm. But Southwell had other plans and instead published a new journal called *The Investigator* which was less shocking to Christian sensibilities. The *Oracle* continued for a short time under the editorship of the less competent Thomas Paterson and soon met its demise.

Paterson and Southwell fell out. Southwell accused Paterson of plagiarism, and after further misadventures the latter emigrated. Maltus Ryall, who gave so much to the cause of Freethought, continued his work for the Anti-Persecution Union and helped Holyoake on the publication of his first journal, *The Movement*. He died in poverty in 1846.

Within a day or two of his release from Gloucester gaol George Jacob Holyoake was lecturing again, and within three months was back in London, now with his younger brother Austin, to set up a publishing house at 147 Fleet Street in emulation of Carlile's at Number 183. Across the street from the Holyoakes' new establishment James Watson, who had published Carlile's early works, had his press. Watson's business seemed to the young Holyoake to be suffering and, feeling guilty at setting up in competition, he sought to remunerated the old man for loss of business.

Holyoake emerged from his imprisonment as a leading figure of the radical, freethinking movement, along with Southwell and another of Southwell's colleagues, Robert Cooper. Temperamentally, Cooper was much like Holyoake, but his convictions were closer to Southwell's with whom he worked on *The Investigator*, and in later years he would challenge Holyoake's leadership. As a coterie they were part of a group of prominent radicals who carried the Owenite banner through the remainder of the decade. It was a losing battle against a disillusionment which overtook the remaining Owenite groups, especially after the failure, through bankruptcy, of the community experiment at Queenswood. The flinty land there had hardly been suitable for agriculture, and its position away from every industrial centre made trade virtually impossible. Before the end, things got so bad that the community committed Owenite heresy by employing local labourers to work the land. The great hall in which the working-class self-helpers had lived, Harmony Hall, was a grandiose affair and was eventually pulled down. The Queenswood estate had been, as Holyoake put it 'a place to look at rather than to live on'.[2] By the 1850s, active and never quite practicable, Owenism had passed away.

Southwell and Holyoake both lectured in Scotland during these years, and Southwell later revived the Hall of Science at Manchester to great effect, but it was the quieter, controlled Holyoake who was accepted as the leading man of the Freethinking movement. Despite his poor voice and lack of strong physical presence, his reputation as a speaker distinguished him from his colleagues, and especially from Southwell. Belief in self-help, which he felt almost as a thing holy, was to remain Holyoake's primary aim: a non-competitive, working class circumvention of the *status quo*, exemplified in the Rochdale cooperative of 1844. But unlike the co-operatives of the north, he would come to accept the usefulness of middle-class funding adopted by the south of England schemes, a practice he had opposed at the time of the fateful lecture at Cheltenham in 1842.

Meanwhile, James Watson put into his young neighbour's head the idea of a weekly periodical to revitalise interest in Freethought, and so, in 1846, *The Reasoner* was born, a paper which Holyoake sold at twopence a copy. Its character was to be communistic, utilitarian, republican and anti-theological.[3] Holyoake thought of it as a way to keep alive Owenism in the minds of his readers. Sales did not cover costs and a fund was started by friends which ensured that he could draw a shilling a week for his pains. Teaching and lecturing brought Holyoake his income.

The paper did, however, work as a catalyst for the activities of various freethinkers. Reports on lectures and discussions on theology which were attended by London-based freethinkers and others from the provinces, and which took place at the City Road Hall of Science, were appended to each issue. And it was in its pages that Holyoake first defined to his public the word secularism, a term he coined. Secularism was his name for a practical morality which 'made the service of others a duty of life' and which efficacy might be 'tested by the experience of this life'.[4] Put simply, secularism was a morality distinct from religious morality. The term, and the Secularist Society which would follow, brought the idea of the acceptability of a morality independent of religion and church authority to the public mind. *The Reasoner* became its voice, Holyoake its leader.

Holyoake had witnessed the start of the Chartist movement in Birmingham in the early 1830s, and he was there in 1848 to see its end following the Kennington Common rally which ended in discord, ridicule and rioting on the streets of London. Theologian and churchman, F.D. Maurice also witnessed the event and was so saddened by the humiliation of the crowd that he spent the whole of the next night with friends writing a manifesto 'To the Working Men of England' from 'A Working Parson'. This group formed itself as the Christian Socialists. Superficially it is reasonable to suppose that Maurice and Holyoake could share intellectual ground. Both pursued a better life for working people, both shared a belief in co-operation, but Holyoake continued to eschew all religious attitudes and would never be a party to Christian Socialist campaigns. He remained one of Maurice's 'un-Christian socialists'.

Prince Albert's Great Exhibition of 1851 drew crowds of every hue and creed to its attractions at Hyde Park, and was a precious first opportunity for the comfortable classes of the manufacturing age to experience, if not within the same social milieu at least while moving under the same roof, the 'rabble', the 'masses', the 'underclasses' of the nation at close quarters and, perhaps, to perceive that this alien group, which demonstrated and rioted for a vote, which smashed machinery and marched for a tolerable life, was not so alien after all. Even so, everyone would be very shocked when the results of a religious census, taken in the same year, showed how uninterested in formal religion the working-classes were. The relevance of Holyoake's secularism movement is illuminated by this revelation. 'The alienation of the people from church and chapel was not founded on lack of spiritual patronage, or thirst for it' he wrote years later, 'but from intellectual dissatisfaction with theological tenets'.[5] The report's author, Horace Mann, put it down to embarrassment at having to sit on benches at the back of the church and through an inability to clothe oneself properly, he blamed it on social rather than intellectual disaffection.

By the 1850s Holyoake had become a respected and well-known figure within and beyond his natural circle, and had working friendships with George Lewes and George Elliot, also with Harriet Martineau and, later, the controversialists Annie Besant and Charles Bradlaugh who became the first declared atheist to take his seat in the House of Commons, although that would not be until 1888. Holyoake tried, three times, for a Common's seat of his own, but each time was unsuccessful. There was a nasty moment, in 1861 when prison threatened for a second time, this time over stamp duty on newpapers, but Gladstone repealed the act and Holyoake escaped a second term behind bars.

As to his friendship with Charles Southwell, it would be nice to think it was one which lasted, but it is hard for a man as outspoken and tactless as Southwell to keep a friend who is as controlled as Holyoake. There certainly is frustration, even a degree of envy, in the sayings and doings of Southwell after their release from prison, which created distance between the two men. He believed that the Holyoake brothers, who had been joined in London by their younger brothers Horatio and Henry, were growing rich by their press, and publicly said so. As the rules of friendship were still binding at this time,

Holyoake privately disabused Southwell of his notion. 'Jacob!' cried Southwell, (he referred to Holyoake as Jacob throughout their years together), 'then you are a damned fool *not* to be making one!'. This was an apology of sorts, but Southwell refused to publicly retract his comments and to Holyoake, always sensitive to any comment which painted him in a false or bad light, this was not forgivable.

The differences in their approaches to debate was such that Southwell could not restrain himself from expressing his anger and disappointment in Holyoake's debating style. To find common ground with your opposite was Holyoake's aim: 'he who cannot find it, cannot convert'.[6] Having gone to prison for the right to hold a view and express it, he felt a moral obligation to extend that right to everyone, opponents included. In debate he believed in giving 'an adversary credit for good faith, you have only to refute his principles – not himself'.[7] Also, he greatly desired not to appear egotistical and so conducted himself in a manner diametrically opposed to Charles Southwell who, being less of an egotist, thought absolutely nothing of such things.

Holyoake disappointed and infuriated Southwell: 'According to my theory, or belief if you will, the Freethinker unprepared to disparage, is unprepared to tell wholesome truth'.[8] When Holyoake debated with the Reverend Brewin Grant on 'Christianity versus Secularism' at the Cowper Street School Room, City Road, over six nights early in 1853, Southwell criticised him for having 'argued throughout as if prepared to accept Christianity in part… as if the scheme of his opponent might be overthrown without disturbing its fundamental assumptions'.[9] Southwell was so plagued by frustration, that the friendship which had led, in part, to Holyoake's imprisonment thirteen years earlier was now as intensely antagonistic as once it had been supportive. Holyoake called Southwell a 'shuffling, inexplicit, ill-worded, disparaging, sarcastic, biting, reproachful, over-bearing and disagreeable sceptic'[10] while Southwell wrote of Holyoake in his 'The Impossibility of Atheism Demonstrated':

> In the art of damaging an opponent, and at the same time concealing from the vulgar eyes his disposition to damage, amid a heap of stereotyped cants about doing the respectable thing, and all manner of petty, curt, sharp, ringing, jaunty, ambiguous, and disjointed sentences about the disagreeableness of disparagement, the excellency of good feeling, good manners, and everything else that is good, Mr Holyoake stands unrivalled – 'himself alone'. [11]

By now Southwell was dismissing the whole matter of religion; for him, atheism had become a useless negation of an irrelevancy. Holyoake's pursuit of a morality called Secularism was of absolutely no interest to him. And there were some who preferred Southwell's approach over Holyoake's. One Mr. Fletcher, a man who sympathised with the aims of the freethinking community, bequeathed him the then huge sum of £30,000. In 1853, or thereabouts, Fletcher changed his will in favour of Holyoake who, in his memoirs, explains this was because Charles Southwell left England for Australia. Unfortunately for Holyoake, Mr. Fletcher, two years later, asked him to come to his house in Kennington where it was revealed that the will had been changed again, this time in favour of Robert Cooper, Southwell's old colleague. It seems a clerk of Holyoake had poisoned Mr. Fletcher's mind against him.[12]

Southwell left England for Australia with the same feelings in his heart as those he had felt when setting sail for Spain – ones of disappointment with life. 'If freethinkers choose to taunt me with inconsistency', he wrote:

> with boxing every point of the speculative compass, or amuse themselves and others by witty sarcasm about my unfortunate disposition to turn and turn, and then go on, and turn again, they are welcome to do so. [13]

He sailed out from Liverpool, on the 22nd of April, 1855, on the *British Trident*. It took almost three months for the 1399 ton vessel to complete its journey to Melbourne, arriving there on the 18th of July. Within four months of his arrival, Southwell was active in the politics of the colony, giving extemporaneous lectures, publishing every week his 'Letters to the People', participating in the vexed land question and putting himself up as a candidate for the Legislative Council. He made friends, but as quickly made enemies.

> There is a person named Southwell who has been endeavouring for sometime to establishing himself as a professional demagogue, and that with a pertinacity that has made him at least a public nuisance. [14]

He turned to the profession his brother Henry had pursued, that is, acting. Southwell joined Foley's touring company and was in Auckland with them in 1856. He wrote from there to Holyoake in the September of that year when it appears their earlier argument was forgotten:

> I expect, ere long, to return to Europe, and familiarise the British public with my experience (dear bought, believe me) in the colonies of Victoria, New South Wales, and New Zealand. Meanwhile I will... from time to time... communicate through you with readers of the Reasoner... some scraps of information concerning things as they *are,* though not exactly as they *ought* to be, in these colonies. [15]

Southwell never did return to Europe. He settled in Auckland to publish his own paper *The Auckland Examiner*, impartial in religious matters, primarily concerned with the politics of the colony, its commerce, shipping, literature and amusements and which competed with *The Southern Cross,* representing the views of the church, and with the Weslyan *The New Zealander*. Nothing would keep him from public debate and his habit of denigrating his opponents' views had not diminished by one degree. It happened that, during a public debate with a local church minister, Mr Hamer, at the Oddfellow's Hall in June, 1856, the tables were turned.

Southwell participated in the debate as a representative of the Freedom of Religion Society which was against state aid of any school in Auckland where religion formed part of the education system.[16] For the occasion Southwell employed an irony so perfect that it was impossible for his hearers to know whether or not he was being sincere. To exclude the Bible as a school book from all schools was, he told his listeners 'very wicked', as there could be no good education imparted without it. The Bible, he said, was the Book of Books, it bound society together and were it to be taken away, the foundations of society would crumble into dust! 'What evil', he asked, 'could befall a boy or girl who used this sacred book as a lesson book in school? Why, nothing whatever; but good would result'.[17] At the end of this speech, Mr Hamer, who must have been stunned and delighted, stood up to say that there was little point in his answering Mr. Southwell's points, and he hoped Mr. Southwell would continue to full acceptance of the Christian faith.

The speech had been a mockery in true Southwellian style and it back-fired on him, badly. The Auckland church paper, *The Southern Cross*, reported on the Southwell and Hamer debate and a story of Charles Southwell's recantation of his Freethinking views was spread. The Holyoake brothers' London press reprinted it in their December 14th issue of the *Reasoner.* 'The whole report', Holyoake wrote,

> may be a joke. If so, it is a very elaborate one, and wears quite the air of reality... If, as we are told, the Holy Spirit is the agent of conversions, it is

> somewhat singular that the New Zealand air should be more favourable to its operations than the atmosphere of London. [18]

Southwell dismissed the whole thing as a nonsense but his friend Robert Cooper was stunned by the report, and *The London Investigator* reported the story of his 'conversion' in January, 1857.

The subject of these reports kept himself busy with the publication of his paper, *The Auckland Examiner*, for four more years, the last two conducted in ill-health. Charles Southwell had succumbed to consumption and he died on August the 7th, 1860, a man of forty-six years, at his home on Symonds Street. He was thought well enough of locally for £200 to be raised for his relief by friends and neighbours in the weeks leading up to his death.

There is no doubting *The Auckland Examiner* was a free press and entirely Southwell's own, but Holyoake inexplicably thought it a Wesleyan publication. He wrote in 1875:

> On the stage, on the platform, or in the secular press he [Southwell] might have found a congenial sphere, but nothing fell to him available except the editorship of a Wesleyan newspaper... When death befell him... he was waited on by members of the proprietory whom he served, to offer him the religious consolations available to that body, and were surprised to be told by their patient that he had edited their paper because no other employment was open to him, but he never undertook to edit their principles. He could not deny that Weslyanism was a form of opinion he could live by, for he had lived by it, and he was much obliged to them for the opportunity of doing that. He, however, preferred to die in his own principles in which he had lived. He was an atheist. [19]

And so the infamous recantation of Charles Southwell never took place.

He was buried in Symonds Street Cemetery. Local freethinkers put-together and erected a fence round his grave, attaching to it the inscription: "He did not become a Wesleyan, nor a preacher, nor editor of a Wesleyan paper".[20] Charles Southwell is remembered in New Zealand to this day as that country's first Freethinker.

17

The Bishop of Exeter did not have his way in everything. His pursuit of the journalist, Thomas Latimer, was to end badly for him. Latimer was a bold man whose pen 'was at its deadliest in contrasting clerical intolerance with clerical rapacity'.[1] As a young man in 1823 he had been deeply impressed by George Birkbeck's speech on self-education, given at the Anchor Tavern in London, and was part of the group which formed the first Mechanics' Institute, of which organisation the *St. James Chronicle* declared 'a scheme more completely adapted for the destruction of this empire could not have been invented by the author of evil himself'.[2] The same fire ran through Latimer's veins as ran through those of men like Holyoake and Southwell. And like Holyoake, Latimer was capable of walking long distances in a short time. He claims he once walked from Exeter to London and back, some three hundred and forty miles, in seven days. And like Southwell, his fearless journalism was a constant prick in the sides of those like Henry Phillpotts.

In 1846 a disagreement came to a head which had been simmering for some years between the Duke of Somerset and the Bishop over the endowment of the church at Berry Pomery. It was shown by the Duke's son, Lord Seymour, that the Bishop had employed 'deliberate falsehood' in the matter. Thomas Latimer promptly reported the damning details in full in the *Western Times*, and in the same issue wrote an editorial in which he said of the Bishop:

> He is so notorious as a brawler, that any story respecting his rule and discipline, provided it do not contain the imputation of any of the milder virtues, is received without question… he stands branded as a consecrated, careless perverter of facts, and one who does no credit to the mitre, which he is paid £200 a week or thereabouts, to wear. [3]

Phillpotts had Latimer indicted for libel and defamation. Purposely to humiliate, he had Latimer cited as a 'labourer' in his indictment, the exact term used to describe George Jacob Holyoake at the time of his trial. As it turned out, the case was not heard until the Lent Assizes of 1848. On the day of the hearing, the Bishop instructed his housekeeper to prepare a victory meal at the Palace for the pleasure of his family and supporters once judgement was made. He was sure of victory and understandably so, the jury comprised eleven Conservatives and only one Liberal. But the Bishop was not a popular man and Latimer had excellent counsel in his friend, Alexander Cockburn who, in his address to the court, drew the issue back to its genesis, the argument between the Duke and Phillpotts in which the latter had undeniably been the wrong-doer. Cockburn turned the argument around on the principle that a journalist has a duty to the public to expose the conduct of public men, that to shrink from it is a dereliction of that duty.

Cockburn ended his address to a burst of spontaneous applause, and when the jury retired to deliberate, an exhausted Latimer left the court, unable to stay another moment in the strained atmosphere. The jury was out too long for the comfort of the prosecution. Their fears were founded, and when Latimer was acquitted the victory cheer in the courtroom was taken up outside and carried through Exeter, the whole process to be repeated in Teignmouth, Torquay and Plymouth as the news travelled.

Had Thomas Latimer had to answer to the Bishop in Holyoake's time, that is before 1843, he would not have left the court a vindicated man, for the veracity, or justification of a disputed statement was not then the issue, only whether it had been said and damaged another's reputation. The Libel Act of 1843 'laid it down that henceforth anyone prosecuted for a defamatory criminal libel would be entitled to plead and prove the truth of the matter'.[4] A nice difference which worked in Latimer's and the press's favour.

The 1843 Act was a sign of the growth in power of a more liberal and secular world. At the time of *Exeter v Latimer*, the Bishop was already indulging in a little further manipulation of another who would prove to be a more famous victim, the Reverend George Cornelius Gorham. When Gorham was appointed as rector to Bramptford Speke, which was in Phillpotts' diocese, the Bishop refused to institute Gorham on the grounds of doctrinal unsoundness over the matter of baptism. Gorham, insisting 'on his right to the rectorship', lost his first legal action against the Bishop which was held at the Court of Arches at Canterbury, but won his appeal through the Judicial Committee of the Privy Council, a secular, not an ecclesiastical, court.[5]

These early signs of what would be an unstoppable process of secularisation of the country's affairs would be anathema to Bishop Phillpotts, who, to quote his official biographer, 'had a full, even extravagant, sense of the dignity and power of the great corporation to which he belonged, and believed it his mission to assert that power to the uttermost'.[6] The Bishop was not alone in his opposition to secular laws overriding ecclesiastical and in his fears for the Established Church. A number of Anglicans turned to Catholicism after the Gorham case, one being H. E. Manning who would go on to support the Dockers' Strike of 1889.

Henry Phillpotts drew his last breath on the 18th of September, 1869, at Bishopstowe. Two years earlier Bishop Wilberforce had paid him a visit and found the old man 'quite himself, but kinder; memory perfect and full of complaisance', adding that it was 'very striking to see the taming of the old lion'.[7] Henry Phillpotts, Bishop of Exeter was buried at St. Mary's, Torquay, having out lived his *bete noire*, Robert Owen, by more than a decade.

* * * * *

It had been seventy years since Owen had visited his native town of Newtown, Monmouthshire, and at the last, and in every sense delivering himself up to his roots, he returned. In October, 1858, a Congress for the Social Sciences was held in Liverpool – an event the eighty-nine year old social reformer could not miss. On the morning of the meeting Owen was vague and poorly. His old friend and colleague, James Rigby, who kept Owen company through his last years, helped him into his clothes and later into the conveyance hired to take him to the hall. It was Lord Brougham who carefully steered the elderly Owen by the arm onto the platform; and to see the 'two marvellous men' stand there, said Holyoake who was there to witness it, was 'a sight not too soon to be beheld again'.[8]

Owen spoke to the gathering as best he could for a man obviously in the last days of his life and Brougham, affected by his old friend's infirmity, quickly brought the address to a close. Owen was returned to the Victoria Hotel and to his bed where he stayed for two weeks. It was now, with just one week left to live, that he decided to make a short visit to Newtown and forthwith set out with James Rigby. For some reason, Owen did not choose to reveal his identity to the people when he arrived there, although it seems that those at the Bear's Head Hotel where he stayed, and the occupiers of the house in which he had been born two doors down, soon understood who their visitor was.

This visit to his home town accomplished, Owen prepared to leave the place and got as far as Shrewsbury, where he took to his bed again. A carriage was hired and he and James Rigby drove back to Newtown and to the Bear's Head Hotel. His son, Robert Dale Owen, was sent for and he arrived on the 16th of November, a day when his father was planning the regeneration of Newtown from his bed. Robert Owen died early the next morning, but not before assuring his son and Mr. Rigby that it was all "very easy and comfortable".[9]

A fog came down across the country, carrying with it a suitable symbolism, and the mourners had to travel through bad and bitterly cold weather for the funeral. George Jacob Holyoake came from London and described the last part of the journey, the road from Shrewsbury to Newtown:

> It was a pleasure to get once more beyond the confines of civilisation, where there were no railroads, and to drive along with smoking horses and blowing bugle, to chat to the guard and treat the coachman, to plunge through the fog, get nipped by the frost… then to draw up under a lamp post and nearly be knocked down, and be knocked up again by a huge mail bag, which the guard threw at you as the best way of getting it on to the coach – then rattling on again, making turnpike keepers start up wildly in their first sleep, run about the road in their shirts to throw open the gates – then dropping small bags of letters on little boys' heads – throwing them over garden walls, and disturbing the whole country as we passed along. [10]

Jacob Bright, Robert Cooper, W H Ashhurst, William Pare, were among those who came to mark Owen's passing. The event took place in fog and frost, in the graveyard of the derelict Saxon church of St. Mary's, and within a few yards of the deep, freezing waters of the Severn river which had nearly claimed his life seven decades before. He was laid where his parents lay, the business passing under the gaze of visitors and dozens of curious local people, young and old. It was a modest affair, made strange by the Rector of St. Mary's insistence that none but he should speak. Holyoake thought it a great shame, when a 'genuine word from the heart of a friend would have been a far holier ceremony'.[11] *

The freezing fog held throughout that day and the next. The mourners' return journey was made through lanes bounded by hoar-frosted trees, each emerging out of the fog 'in its bright and sparking glory, like a bride'.[12] This is apposite imagery from Holyoake, for although Owen's ideas for a better world were considered hopelessly utopian by friends, debauched and dangerous by his enemies, he never doubted their eventual adoption by government, that is; education for all; humane conditions and proper remuneration for workers; abolition of child labour; the separation of state policies from religious interests; international arbitration; and equitable distribution of wealth. Frozen trees awaiting a future spring.

* Richard Carlile's interment, in consecrated ground at Kensal Green Cemetery, had also been marred by the appearance of a cleric who asserted his authority by reciting the Church service over the grave. In Carlile's case, his son Richard objected and eventually left the scene.

Epilogue

On a Sunday evening in May, 1854, George Jacob Holyoake walked with his mother to John Angell James' Congregational Chapel on Carrs Lane. He thought its service might console her after the recent death of her husband and he entered the building for the first time in seventeen years:

> What vicissitudes of religious experiences had I gone through since I last walked along its familiar galleries! What an utter, an unforeseen change had my life undergone since then! There was the well-known clock, whose tardy hands I had watched often wearily from the Sunday-school gallery, and the organ with its monotonous peals... There, also, I recognised a face almost in every pew which I had known before – faces I never saw smile, and which now looked as though they had never smiled since we met before. How should those who read believingly the "Anxious Inquirer" ever smile? [1]

As fate would have it, John Angell James was not preaching at Carrs Lane that night, and Holyoake missed an opportunity to hear again his splendid voice and evangelical sentiments summoning the ways of a time already past for some. John Angell James died five years later and was buried beneath his beloved pulpit where he lay until the building was demolished. His remains were moved and are now lost in an unmarked grave.

George Jacob Holyoake did not see himself as a martyr, and martyrdom was not his motivation at the time of his trial in 1842. From early manhood he held his own dignity and worth, in the eyes of others, as very precious, and he believed absolutely in his own moral code. He freely admits to possessing a vengeful nature and to a dread of being thought egotistical because, in all likelihood, he knew it was his failing. He was too much of an egotist to be a martyr. It was outraged morality, wounded pride and good deal of courage which accompanied his steps in 1842.

In his later years, he is described by a member of the Leicester Secular Society as a 'dignified and picturesque figure. He had the clear pink and white complexion of a child, flowing, wavy, silver white hair, white moustache and small pointed beard, with shaven cheeks. In winter time [he wore] a voluminous fur lined overcoat which seemed to be almost too heavy for his small and seemingly fragile body to carry'.[2]

He was to outlive most of his contemporaries, all twelve of his siblings and his wife Ellen, who died in 1884. In 1855, his seven-year-old son Max was killed in a traffic accident in London, and fifty-three years after Madeline's death he had a brass plate cut to mark her resting place. He always said Madeline had 'perished', a term borrowed from Evangelical vocabulary: 'There is a world of misery in that word. Perish', John Angell James had written. Madeline, the innocent in this story, had perished in a temporal world of hardships reserved for people of the working classes.

George Jacob Holyoake died on the 22nd of January, 1906, three months before entering his ninetieth year and very shortly after enjoying the excitement of a General Election which brought in a victorious Liberal government as well as twenty-nine nominees of the Labour Representation Committee which eventually would result in a parliamentary Labour party. What must he have felt at that? Holyoake had started out in days when rich and poor were designated so by Divine Providence and he lived to see a growing challenge to this notion, a social change in which he played a significant part. He witnessed the emergence of a social gospel led by the Birmingham non-conformist minister George Dawson who preached municipal responsibility towards the poor and which cause was taken up by R. W. Dale, John Angell James' successor at Carrs Lane. What was called 'honest doubt' was publicly admitted by some in the Anglican Church. Some clergy and an increasing number of the laity could no longer subscribe to a vicarious atonement as they saw it, nor to the idea of hell for those who could not believe, and said so.

George Jacob Holyoake was buried at Highgate Cemetery close to the graves of George Henry Lewes and George Eliot. His motto for the mundane world was 'avoid excess in food, in pleasure, in work, and in expectation'.[3] He thought the best of himself and others, believing that consciously to do so is one of humankind's finest endowments. As to death, he saw its terrors as 'the rod whereby [priests] whip the understanding into submission to untenable dogmas'.[4] Christ had preached the moral 'do unto others as you would have them do unto you', and so, along with a growing number of Christians, he dismissed as contrary to this moral any notion of a divine father who would condemn a soul to the outer darkness or worse. He did not fear death. 'Nothing', he wrote, 'can disturb the peace of mind of those armed by a fortitude founded on love and justice, on rectitude and reason'.[5]

Bibliography: Primary Sources

UNPUBLISHED MANUSCRIPTS AND SOURCES:

1) Holyoake, G. J., *Log Book 1*; *Self-Culture, Uses of Books Brief Notes on Lectures 1838-9*; held at Bishopsgate Institute, London
2) Register of Prisoners, Summer Assizes at Gloucester Q/Gc 5/7; Prison's Calendars 1842, held at Gloucester
3) Letters held at The Cooperative Union Library, Holyoake House, Hanover Street, Manchester and on fiche at Birmingham Archives
4) Robert Owen Collection, The Cooperative Union Library, Holyoake House, Hanover Street, Manchester

NEWSPAPERS:

Cheltenham Chronicle 1842, at Cheltenham Reference Library
Cheltenham Free Press 1842, at Cheltenham Reference Library
Cheltenham Journal 1842, at Cheltenham Reference Library
Gloucester Journal 1842, at Gloucester Records Office
New Moral World 1839-1842, at Birmingham Central Library
Oracle of Reason 1842, at the British Library

BOOKS:

Bentley (1840) *History of Worcestershire*
Close, Francis (1826) *Introductory Sermon preached at the Parish Church of Cheltenham*
Close, Francis (1839) *A Sermon addressed to the Chartists of Cheltenham*, Hamilton, Adams & Co., London
Close, France (1839a) *A Sermon address to the Female Chartists of Cheltenham*, Hamilton, Adams & Co, London
Close, Francis (1853) *Table Turning not Diabolical*, Hamilton, Adams & Co.
Cobbett, William (1912), *Rural Rides*, J M Dent & Sons Ltd
Dale, R.W. (18..) *Life and Letters of John Angell James including an unfinished autobiography*, James Nisbet and Co, London

Davis, Henry (1843) *Cheltenham in its past and present state*

Edwards, E (1877) *Personal Recollections of Birmingham and Birmingham Men*, Midland Educational Trading Company Limited

English Historical Documents 1815-70, Methuen

Evangelical Alliance (1859) *History and Prospectus of the Evangelical Alliance*

Gimson, Sydney A, (1932) *Random Recollections of the Leicester Secular Society, with Digressions*, Part 1, (held at Leicester Records Office)

Granville, A. B., (1841) *Spars of England, Midland Spas*

Greville, C. C. (1885) *A Journal of the Reign of Queen Victoria, from 1837 to 1852*, Vols I & II, Longmans, Green and Co

Holyoake, G. J. *Paley Refuted in his Own Words*

Holyoake, G. J. *Practical Grammar* (A.425 Birmingham Library Archives)

Holyoake, G. J. (1838) *Report of George Jacob Holyoake, J Rabone and D Baker regarding the comets of Birmingham*, Birmingham Library Archives (Ref: 589884)

Holyoake, G. J. (1842) *The Spirit of Bonner in the disciples of Christ*

Holyoake, G. J. (1851) *History of the last Trial by Jury for Atheism in England*, James Watson, London

Holyoake, G. J. (1855) *Life and Character of Richard Carlile*, (A320-8 e/41 Birmingham Library Archives)

Holyoake, G. J. (1859) *Life and Last Days of Robert Owen*, (A335.08. D/3 Birmingham Library Archives)

Holyoake, G. J. (1870a) *The Logic of Death*, Austin & Co

Holyoake, G. J. (1870b) *The Logic of Life*, Austin & Co

Holyoake, G. J. (1879) *Secularism, Scepticism and Atheism*, Austin & Co

Holyoake, G. J. (1874) *The Limits of Atheism*, J A Brook & Co

Holyoake, G. J. (1893) *Sixty Years of an Agitator's Life*, Vols I & II, London, T Fisher Unwin

Holyoake, G. J. (1895) *Public Speaking and Debate*, T. Fisher Unwin

Holyoake, G. J. (1905) *Bygones Worth Remembering*, T Fisher Unwin

Hunt, (1842) *The Trial of George Jacob Holyoake on the indictment for Blasphemy*,

James, J. A. (1835) *The Anxious Inquirer after Salvation*, Religious Tract Society

James, J. A. (1845) *Pastoral Addresses*

Jones, Lloyd (1900) *The Life, Times, and Labours of Robert Owen*, (Third edition) Swan Sonnenschein & Co. Ltd

Knapp (1830) *Journal of a Naturalist*, John Murray, London

Linton, W. J. (1800) *James Watson, A Memoir*, in Neuburg, Victor E. (1971) *Literacy & Society*, Woburn Press

Memorials to Dean Close. Edited by one who knew him *(1885). George Rivers. Held at British Library.*

Mill, John Stuart (1873) *Autobiography*, Penguin Classics edition

Owen, Robert (1817) *Report to the Committee of the Association for the Relief of the Manufacturing and Labouring Poor*

Owen, Robert (1840) *Lectures on the Marriages of the Priesthood* A335.08 D/3 Birmingham

Owen, Robert (1840a) *The Book of the New Moral World*, H Robinson & Co.

Owen, Robert (1841) *Lectures on the Rational System of Society*, Home Colonial Society

Owen, Robert, *Public Discussion between Robert Owen and Mr John Brindley* A335.08 D/3 Birmingham

Owen, Robert (1857) *Life of Robert Owen, by himself*, Charles Knight & Co Ltd

Paine, Thomas (1794) *The Age of Reason*, Gramercy Books, New York

Paine, Thomas, *The Rights of Man*

Philosophic Society (1838) *Report of George Jacob Holyoake, J Rabone and D Baker regarding the comets of Birmingham* (held in Birmingham Archives)

Pigot Trade Register, Gloucestershire 1842

Pitt, W (1813) *General View of the Agriculture of the County of Worcester*, Sherwood, Neely, and Jones

Smith, James Elishama (1840) *The Little Book, or Momentous Crisis of 1840* Birmingham Library, Social Sciences D 208 C/9

Southwell, Charles (1840) *An Essay on Marriage, addressed to the Lord Bishop of Exeter*

Southwell, Charles, *Confessions of a Freethinker*

Bibliography: Secondary Sources

Ackroyd, Peter (2002) *London, the Biography*, Chatto and Windus
Aldred, Guy A. (1941) *Richard Carlile Agitator, His Life and Times*, Strickland Press, Glasgow
Blaszak, Barbara J (1988) *George Jacob Holyoake (1817-1906) and the Development of the British Cooperative Movement*, The Edwin Mellen Press
Brook, C.W. (1943) *Carlile and the Surgeons*, A320.8 e/41
Butt, John (ed) (1971) *Robert Owen, Prince of Cotton Spinners*, David and Charles, Newton Abbot
Chaloner, W.H. (1954) *Robert Owen, Peter Drinkwater and the Early Factory System in Manchester 1788-1800*
Chinn, Carl (1995) *Poverty amidst prosperity, The urban poor in England, 1834-1914*, Manchester University Press
Claeys, Gregory (1987) *Machinery, Money and the Millennium*, Polity Press in association with Basil Blackwell
Claeys, Gregory (1989) *Citizens and saints, politics and anti-politics in early British socialism*, Cambridge University Press
Claeys, Gregory, ed (1993) *Selected Works of Robert Owen*, Vol 1, William Pickering
Clayre, A. (ed) (1977) *Nature & Industrialization*, Oxford Press in association with Open University
Clune, Harold P. *The Face of London*, Spring Books
Davies, G.C.B., (1954) *Henry Phillpotts, Bishop of Exeter, 1778-1869*, S.P.C.K.
Dent, R.K. (1880) *Old and New Birmingham*
Dent, R.K. (1973) *Old and New Birmingham*, republished by EP Publishing
Dodds, John W. (1953) *The Age of Paradox*, Victor Gallancz Ltd
Froude, J.A. (1884) *Thomas Carlyle, a History of his Life in London* Vol 1, Longmans, Green, & Co.
Gaut, R.C., *A History of Worcestershire Agriculture* (Malvern)
Glasby, Jon, (1999) *Poverty and Opportunity, 100 years of the Birmingham Settlement*, Brewin Books
Glover, Richard (1884) under the pseudonym Ignotus Contem, *The Golden Decade of a Favored Town*, Elliot Stock, London

Grugel, Lee E. (1976) *George Jacob Holyoake*, Porcupine Press, Philadelphia
Gwilliam, Bill, (1991) *Worcestershire's Hidden Past*, Halfshire Books
Hammond, J.L. & Barbara Hammond (1962) *The Age of the Chartists 1832-1854, A Study of Discontent*, Archon Books, Hamden Connecticut
Hopkins, Eric (1989) *Birmingham, The First Manufacturing Town in the World*, Weidenfeld & Nicolson
Huch, Ronald K. (1993) *Henry, Lord Brougham, The Later Years 1830-1868*, The Edwin Mellen Press
Hudson, W.H. *Birds in London* in Massingham, Hugh & Pauline
Jurica, John (1994) *Gloucester, A Pictorial History*, Phillimore
Karl, Frederick, (1995) *George Eliot, a Biography*, Harper Collins
Keep, H.F., *History of Carrs Lane* in Congregational Historical Society Transactions Vol 9, Birmingham
Lambert, Richard S. (1939) *The Cobbett of the West*, Nicholson and Watson, London
Leapman, M. (ed), *The Book of London*, Weidenfeld and Nicolson
London History Atlas (1997) The Times
Long, P.J. and W.V. Awdry, (1987) *The Birmingham and Gloucester Railway*, Alan Sutton
Malcolmson, R.W. (1981) *Life and Labour in England 1700-1780*, Hutchinson
Massingham, Hugh & Pauline, *The London Anthology*, Spring Books
McCabb, J. (1908) *Life and Letters of George Jacob Holyoake*, Watts & Co, London
Norman, Andrew (2008) *The Story of George Loveless and the Tolpuddle Martyrs*, Halsgrove
Oxford Dictionary of National Biography, (2004), Oxford University Press
Parsons (ed) (1988) *Religion in Victorian Britain, Controversies*, Manchester University Press in association with the Open University
Pearce, H.H. (1957) *New Zealand Rationalist: Charles Southwell in Australia and New Zealand*, (at the British Library)
Perry, R. (1986) *Wotton-under-Edge, Times Past – Time Present*, Paines Associates.
Podmore, Frank, (1906) *Robert Owen, a biography*, George Allen & Unwin Ltd
Richardson, John (1995) *London & Its People*, Barrie & Jenkins
Roach, John (1978) *Social Reform in England*
Royle, Edward (1974) *Victorian Infidels: the origins of the British Secularist Movement 1791-1866*, Manchester University Press, Rowman and Littlefield

Royle, Edward, (1980) *Chartism*, Longman

Shutte, R.N. (1863) *Life, Times and Writings of the Right Rev. Dr Henry Phillpotts*, Saunders, Otley, and Co.

Stevenson, J. & R. Quinault, (1974) *Popular Protest and Public Order, Six Studies in British History, 1790-1920*, George Allen & Unwin Ltd

Thomas, William (1979) *The Philosophic Radicals: Nine Studies in Theory and Practice, 1817-1841*, Clarendon Press

Thompson, Brian (2004) *Devastating Eden, The Search for Utopia in America*, Harper Collins

Trafford, R.S. (1997) *The Rev. Francis Close and the Foundation of the Training Institution at Cheltenham 1843-78*

Vanstone, W.H. (1977) *Love's Endeavour. Love's Expense*, Darton, Longman & Todd

Victoria History of the County of Gloucestershire, Oxford University Press

Vidler, Alec R. (1966) *F.D. Maurice and Company*, SCM Press Ltd

Village Atlas, The, (1989) *The Growth of Birmingham and the West Midlands 1831-1907*, The Alderman Press

Wilson, A.N. (1999) *God's Funeral*, John Murray

Wilson, A.N. (2002) *The Victorians*, Hutchinson, London

Woodward, E.L. (1938) *The Age of Reform 1815-1870*, Oxford History of England

Notes

Chapter One

1. Holyoake (1842) p.4
2. Holyoake (1842) p.26
3. Holyoake (1893) Vol 1. p.4
4. Thomas, p.43
5. Holyoake (1893) Vol 1, p.4
6. J. B.Bebbington in 'Propagandist' 3 May, 1862, quoted in Pearce
7. Grugel, p.19
8. Oracle of Reason No. 4
9. Quoted in Royle (1974), p.75-6
10. Holyoake (1842), pp.6 & 7
11. Holyoake (1993), Vol 1, p.11
12. Holyoake (1993), Vol 1, pp.61-2
13. Letters, No. 3 August 1838
14. Holyoake (1893) Vol 1, p.65

Chapter Two

1. quoted in Karl p.53
2. *ibid* p.134
3. Pitt, W, (1813) pp.185-6
4. *ibid* pp.138-9
5. quoted in Dale, R. W. (1861) p.90
6. Dent p.363
7. Dale (1861) p.97
8. Keep p.57
9. James J. A. (1835), p.29
10. *ibid*, pp.28 and 29
11. Dale (1861) p.15
12. *ibid* p.33
13. *ibid* p.52
14. *ibid* p.132
15. Edwards p.18
16. Keep p.59
17. in McCabe p.517
18. Holyoake (1893) Vol 1 p.69
19. *ibid* p.71
20. Letters, No. 7
21. Holyoake (1893) Vol 1 p.75
22. Holyoake, Brief Notes on Lectures (unpaged) held at Bishopsgate Institute
23. *ibid*

Chapter Three

1. Log Book 1, held at Bishopsgate Institute
2. *Self Culture, Uses of Books,* held at Bishopsgate Institute
3. James (1835) p.24
4. *ibid*, p.1
5. *ibid*, p.44
6. Pitt, W., (1813), p.21-2
7. Holyoake, (1870b), p.4
8. Holyoake (1905), p.218-19
9. *ibid,* p.228-9
10. Holyoake, (1870a) p.7
11. *ibid*, p.12
12. Holyoake (1893), Vol II, p.384
13. Holyoake (1838) *Report of George Jacob Holyoake, J Rabone and D Baker*, held at Birmingham Archives

Chapter Four

1. quoted in Claeys, ed (1993), p.216
2. *Hansard*, quoted in Malcolmson (1981)
3. Holyoake, (1893) Vol I, p.83-4
4. Dent, R.K., (1973) p.456.
5. James Jaffray quoted in Dent (1973) p.457
6. Holyoake, (1893) Vol I, p.84
7. Edwards, E. (1877) pp.29-31
8. Holyoake *ibid*
9. Edwards, *ibid*

Chapter Five

1. Owen (1857), p.xxxvii
2. *ibid*, p.9
3. *ibid*, pp.15-16

4. *ibid*, p.19
5. *ibid*, p.25
6. Bulletin of John Rylands Library Vol 37, No. 1, 1954
7. Owen (1857), p.7
8. in Jones, Lloyd (1900), p.60
9. Owen (1857), pp.112-13
10. Jones, Lloyd (1900), p.37
11. *Book of the New Moral World* p.47
12. James, J. A. (1835), p.29
13. Owen (1857), pp.104-5
14. *ibid*
15. quoted in Holyoake (1859) pp.19-20

Chapter Six

1. Jones, Lloyd (1900), p.114
2. *ibid*, quoted, p.120
3. Thompson, Brian (2004), gives an excellent account of New Harmony's history.
4. quoted in Holyoake, (1859), p.19
5. Stevenson, pp.186-7
6. Roach, p.26
7. Norman, p.149
8. Holyoake (1870a) *Logic of Death*, p.4
9. Cobbett (1912), pp.120 & 268
10. Holyoake, (1893), Vol I, p.133
11. *ibid*, p.188
12. in *The New Moral World*, 16.01.1841
13. quoted in Royle (1974), p.77
14. quoted in *The New Moral World*, Vol 9, p.87
15. Pitt, W. (1813), pp.8-9
16. quoted in Grugel, Lee E. (1976), p.21
17. Pitt, W. (1813), p.268

Chapter Seven

1. Holyoake, (1893) Vol I, p.146
2. Cobbett (1912), pp.33-4. See also Granville (1841) pp.316 & 231
3. Thomas (1979) p.58
4. Cobbett, (1912) p.112
5. Pitt, W. (1813), p.316
6. see Granville's chapter on Cheltenham
7. Glover, Richard (1884), p.32-3
8. *ibid*, p.20
9. *ibid* p.32-3
10. *ibid* p.27
11. *ibid* p.20
12. Close, Francis (1826), p.11-12
13. *ibid*, pp.13 & 22
14. Close, Francis, (1839a), pp.25-6

Chapter Eight

1. Davies p.18
2. Lambert, p.35
3. Greville, quoted in David, p.328
4. Davis, p.21
5. quoted in Davis, pp.18-19
6. Davis p.138, 139-40
7. *ibid*, p.144
8. Robert Owen Collection, Manchester, 30 (2)
9. New Moral World Jan 24, 1840, (p.1073-4, held at Birmingham Archives)
10. Huch, p.2
11. quoted in Davis, p.338
12. *New Moral World* January 24 1840, (p.1007 held at Birmingham Archives)
13. Southwell (1840) p.3 & p.9

Chapter Nine

1. taken from 'Notes Taken on Night of Blasphemy' letter No. 44 (MM96636/1) (Manchester)
2. the whole of this passage is taken from Holyoake (1851) and Hunt (1842)
3. *The New Moral World*, 1841, p.119 (Birmingham)
4. Letter No. 32
5. Hunt (1842) pp.22-3

Chapter Ten

1. Letter No. 28, MI:39, March 1842, Manchester
2. Southwell *Confessions* p.70
3. *ibid*, p.5-6
4. *ibid*, p.6
5. *ibid*, p.13

6. *ibid*, p.14
7. *ibid*, p.9
8. *ibid*, p.15
9. Letter No. 36 (Reel 335.1942, 3.4.42)
10. Southwell *Confessions*, p.29
11. *ibid*, p.35
12. Holyoake (1893), Vol 1, p.300
13. Southwell *ibid*, pp.35-6
14. letter No. 36
15. Southwell, *Confessions*, p.38
16. Southwell *Confessions*, p.48
17. *ibid*, p.50
18. *ibid*, p.54
19. Richardson, p.158
20. Southwell *Confessions*, p.58
21. *The New Moral World*, Jan 25 1840

Chapter Eleven

1. Details of this Congress are taken from *The New Moral World* 1841, pp.316-17
2. Somerville, in Dodd, p.181
3. Southwell, *Confessions* p.63-4
4. *New Moral World*, June 6 issue, 1841
5. *New Moral World*, May 13, 1842
6. Holyoake, (1893), p.143
7. Holyoake, (1851), p.7
8. *ibid*, pp.6-7
9. *The Oracle of Reason* March 26, 1842, quoted in Royle 1974
10. Letter No. 28 MI:39, March 1842
11. Holyoake, (1842a), p.32

Chapter Twelve

1. quoted in Dodd p.92
2. Letter No. 51, (M1:70)
3. Holyoake (1893) Vol 1 p.152
4. Holyoake (1905) p.240
5. Hunt (1842), p.16
6. Holyoake (1851) p.8
7. *Cheltenham Free Press* (1842) p.181
8. Holyoake (1851) p.8
9. the section on Holyoake's arrest is taken from *Cheltenham Chronicle* June 6, (1842)
10. Holyoake (1851) pp.8-10
11. *ibid*, p.11
12. Holyoake (1893) Vol 1 p.169
13. Holyoake (1851) pp.15-16
14. Letters, No. 47
15. Letters, No. 49
16. Mill, J. S. (1873), p.123
17. Thomas, p.209
18. Holyoake (1893) p.153
19. Holyoake (1851) p.16

Chapter Thirteen

1. McCabb p.32
2. Holyoake (1893), pp.87-8
3. *Northern Star & Leeds General Advertiser*, Sat, August 6, 1842, Issue 247
4. Holyoake, (1851) p.17
5. Thomas Carlyle, quoted in Froude (1884), p.187
6. Dodd, p.234
7. Letters, No. 49, microfiche held at Birmingham Archives
8. Letters, No. 57, microfiche held at Birmingham Archives
9. Holyoake, (1893) Vol 1, p.154-6
10. *ibid*, p.187
11. Holyoake (1855), page v, (Preface)
12. Holyoake (1893) Vol 1, p.187
13. quoted in Aldred, Chapter XXVII
14. Letters, No. 59, microfiche held at Birmingham Archives
15. in Parsons (1988), p.281
16. in Aldred, p.20
17. *ibid*, p.21
18. *ibid*
19. *ibid*, p.52
20. *ibid*, pp.52-3
21. *ibid*, p.54
22. *ibid*, pp.60-1
23. quoted in Shutte, p.47
24. in Aldred, p.61

Chapter Fourteen

1. *Cheltenham Free Press*, May 21, 1842, p.164

2. Royle, E., (1974), p.80
3. Letters, No. 58
4. Holyoake (1851) p.17
5. Letters, No. 58
6. Holyoake (1893) Vol 1, 156
7. Letters, August 14, 1842 and 60 years p.188
8. Hunt (1842), pp.1-2
9. *ibid*, p.7
10. *ibid* pp.5-6
11. Letters, No. 60
12. Register of Prisoners, Assizes Q/Gc 5/7, held at Gloucester Records Office
13. Holyoake (1893) p.163 and Holyoake (1851) p.21
14. Letters 62, August 14, 1842
15. Holyoake (1851), p.19
16. *ibid*, p.20
17. *ibid*, p.97
18. Holyoake (1895), p.27
19. Holyoake (1893) Vol 1, p.158
20. details for the passages relating to the trial are mainly taken from Hunt (1842) and *Cheltenham Chronicle*, August 20, 1842
21. Hunt (1842) p.3
22. *ibid*, p.18
23. *ibid*, p.19
24. *ibid*, p.30 and p.33
25. *ibid*, p.36
26. *ibid*, p.45
27. *ibid*, p.67
28. *ibid*, pp.65-68
29. Holyoake (1842), p.4

Chapter Fifteen

1. quoted in Stevenson, J, and R. Quinault (1974), p.155
2. Dale, R. W., p.397
3. *ibid*, pp.399-400
4. *ibid*, p.401
5. Holyoake (1842), p.4
6. Holyoake (1893) Vol 1, p.166-7
7. Letters, Aug 24, 1842, microfiche held at Birmingham Archives
8. Holyoake (1851), p.26
9. Letters, No. 66, microfiche held at Birmingham Archives
10. Carlile's letter to Erskine, Aug 23, quoted in *The Oracle of Reason*
11. Letters, Aug 20, 1842
12. Holyoake, (1893) Vol 1, p.167
13. Holyoake's Log Book 1, Aug 22 and Letters No.63
14. Holyoake (1855), p.28
15. in Aldred, p.142
16. Holyoake (1893) Vol 1, p.172
17. Holyoake, *Paley Refuted in his Own Words*, p.37
18. Letters, Oct 14, 1842
19. Holyoake's Log Book 1, Oct 18
20. Letters Nos. 87, MM96636/1
21. Letters No. 83
22. Holyoake (1893) Vol 1, p.176
23. *Oracle of Reason,* Aug 1842, p.327
24. Letters, No. 88, Dec 11, 1842
25. Holyoake (1893) Vol 1, p.173
26. quoted in Dobbs, pp.103-4
27. Holyoake (1893) Vol 1, p.168
28. in Aldred, p.124
29. *ibid*, p.55

Chapter Sixteen

1. Greville p.136
2. quoted in Blazak, p.43
3. see Royle (1974), pp.92-3
4. quoted in Blazak, p.21
5. Holyoake (1905), pp.86-7
6. Holyoake (1895), p.48
7. *ibid*, p.54
8. quoted in Pearce, Dec 1957, p.7
9. *ibid*, Nov 1957, p.8
10. *ibid*, Nov 1957, p.7
11. *ibid*
12. Holyoake (1893), pp.69-70
13. Charles Southwell's *Impossibility of Atheism*, quoted in Pearce Nov, 1957, p.6
14. *The Age* quoted in Pearce, June 1957, p.8

15. *The Reasoner* No. 561, quoted in Pearce, 1st March 1957
16. quoted in Pearce, May 1957, p.9
17. quoted in Pearce, February 1958, p.12
18. *The Reasoner* No. 550, (quoted in Pearce, Dec 14, 1956)
19. Holyoake, *History of Cooperation*, quoted in Pearce, Sept 1957, p.8
20. Pearce, Aug 1957, p.9

Chapter Seventeen

1. Lambert, p.108
2. quoted in Lambert, p.21
3. *ibid*, pp.138 and 139-40
4. *ibid*, p.145
5. Parsons (ed), p.96
6. Davies, p.38
7. in Davies, p.384
8. Holyoake (1859), p.7
9. *ibid*, p.10
10. *ibid*, pp.10-11
11. *ibid* p.27, (A335.08. D/3 Birmingham Library Archives)
12. *ibid*, p.15

Epilogue

1. Holyoake (1893) Vol 1 p.13
2. Gimson, Sydney A.
3. Holyoake (1905) p.240
4. Holyoake (1870a), p.12
5. *ibid*, p.13

Index

Index Notes: second-level subheadings which deal with biographical detail are listed in chronological order. GJH refers to George Jacob Holyoake; CS refers to Charles Southwell.